LOST
FLINT

LOST
FLINT

GARY FLINN

THE
History
PRESS

Published by The History Press
Charleston, SC
www.historypress.com

Copyright © 2021 by Gary Flinn
All rights reserved

First published 2021

Manufactured in the United States

ISBN 9781467144926

Library of Congress Control Number: 2021931015

In memory of the hundreds of Genesee County residents who have died of COVID-19.

CONTENTS

Preface: Things Not Here Anymore   9
Acknowledgements   13

PART I. FLINT'S GROWTH   15
How Flint Developed   15
Lost to Progress   17
Lost to Disasters   26
Lost to Neglect   30
Lost Neighborhoods to "Progress"   33
The White Flight to the Suburbs   39

PART II. FLINT'S DECLINE   41
Lost to the University of Michigan–Flint Downtown Campus   41
Lost to "Progress"   44
Lost to Water Street Pavilion   47
Lost to the Ill-Fated AutoWorld   52
Lost to Neglect   54
They Didn't Build High-Rises in the 1960s Like They Used To   55
Lost Industry   59
More Lost Industries   67
Lost Media   73
Lost Traditions   79
Lost Schools   81

Contents

Lost Hospitals 84
Lost Houses of Worship 86
Lost Commercial Strips 98
Lost to Neglect 107
Lost Neighborhoods 114
North of Downtown: A Tale of Two Adjacent Redevelopments 122
Loss of Control 125
The Flint Water Crisis Aftermath 127

PART III. HOPE FOR THE FUTURE
Redeveloping Buick City 131
Downtown Flint Developments 133
Improvements to Berston Field House 143
Communities First Offers Quality Affordable Housing 145
Clark Commons Breathing New Life to Smith Village 148

Appendix 151
Bibliography 163
Index 169
About the Author 173

Preface

THINGS NOT HERE ANYMORE

When I was asked by my The History Press editor, John Rodrigue, to write my third book, titled *Lost Flint*, I recalled a pair of television specials produced in 1995 and 1997 by WKAR-TV, the PBS station serving the Lansing area, owned and operated by Michigan State University. The program was titled *Things Not Here Anymore*, and it was about places and things that no longer exist in the Lansing area. To assist in formatting the *Lost Flint* book, Rodrigue sent me a title called *Lost Gary, Indiana* by Jerry Davich. While there were parallels between what happened to Flint and what happened to the United States Steel company town of Gary, the two industrial cities are like comparing apples to oranges. Gary was indeed a company town developed by United States Steel around its steel mill and was incorporated in 1909, making it a much newer town compared to Flint, which was incorporated as a city in 1855. Flint was an ideal overland stopping point for travelers between Detroit and Saginaw and during the latter part of the nineteenth century was a major lumbering town with a few lumber mills. Lumbering led to the development of the carriage industry, which gave Flint the nickname of the Vehicle City. The carriage industry evolved into the automotive industry, which gave Flint its rapid growth in the first half of the twentieth century.

In making comparisons between Flint, Lansing and Gary, three downtown landmarks expressed what happened to these places. These are all classic downtown movie palaces from the 1920s, designed by world-renowned theater architect John Eberson. They are the Michigan Theatre in Lansing, the Palace Theatre in Gary and the Capitol Theatre in Flint. All three were closed as first-run movie theaters by 1980—the Palace in Gary in 1972, the Capitol in Flint in 1976 and the Michigan in Lansing in 1980. Sadly, the Palace in Gary deteriorated over time and now is so badly damaged by vandalism, disrepair and neglect that I fear it is beyond saving. On the other hand, the front façade of the Michigan Theatre building, arcade and lobby were restored in the 1980s, and it is now the Atrium Building. Sadly, most of the theater itself was torn down in 1983. After the Capitol Theatre in Flint closed, it was sold to the Farah family in 1977, and while there were attempts over the years to revive the theater, it was put in mothballs because the heating system broke down beyond repair in 1996. While the storefront and office areas of the theater building were still in use, the theater was kept in repair until it was sold to a nonprofit developer in 2015. It was beautifully restored to its 1928 appearance and reopened in 2017.

While the first part of the book is about the places Flint lost while it was a growing city, the much thicker second part of the book is about the places Flint lost during its decline from the 1970s to the Flint Water Crisis that began in 2014. The last part of this book, titled "Hope for the Future," is about the positive things that happened in the city of Flint in recent years.

While my first two books, *Remembering Flint, Michigan* and *Hidden History of Flint*, were mostly adapted from previously published articles, this book is my first book written from the ground up. About halfway into writing the text, the COVID-19 pandemic hit. While the Flint Public Library had closed at the end of February to prepare for renovations, the temporary relocation to the Courtland Center mall in Burton was delayed into the summer as a result of the pandemic. The closing of other area libraries forced this writer to rely on sources from the internet, as well as reader suggestions posted on my books' Facebook page. While this was going on, I was asked to review a new book by Kyle Brooky, titled *Abandoned Flint*, which visually describes various abandoned places in and around Flint. This also gave me ideas regarding what to include in this book. In August 2020, when the Flint Public Library reopened its reference section at the temporary Courtland Center location, all of the books had to wait up to a week for sanitizing before being returned to shelves. That limited what I could use for research material. Lesser-used volumes were put into storage outside the library and were thus inaccessible even to library staff.

Along with the people in the acknowledgments that follow, I want to also thank Ivonne, who met me because of my first book and helped me with both my second book and this book.

Gary Flinn
February 2021

ACKNOWLEDGEMENTS

Thanks to the YMCA of Greater Flint.

Thanks to readers of the Flint Expatriates website (http://www.flintexpats.com) for their memories of Paramount Potato Chips.

Thanks to the families of DuPont Flint plant workers who contributed their memories to the You Know You're from Flint Facebook page.

Thanks to Mike Brandt and Anthony Morey for their recollections of the church when it was First Church of the Nazarene.

Thanks to the various contributors who nominated churches in the Facebook page for my books.

Thanks to Congregation Beth Israel and Temple Beth El.

Thanks to followers of my books' Facebook page, as well as followers of the Kearsley High School and Holy Rosary Memories Album Facebook page for their recollections, which supplemented my own memories of Thompson's Shopping Center.

Thanks to Bryant Nolden for sharing future plans regarding Berston Field House.

Thanks to Joel Rash and others who shared their recollections about Windmill Place.

Thanks to David White, the Carriage Town Historic Neighborhood Association and input from various Flint History pages on Facebook.

Thanks to Felicia Naimark for her input regarding the lost schools.

Along with the staff of the Flint Public Library, I would especially like to thank Flint expatriate and California resident Wendy All for her input.

Part I

FLINT'S GROWTH

How Flint Developed

The location of Flint was originally a break on the Saginaw Trail from Detroit to Saginaw that was created by the Flint River. That location was called the Grand Traverse. The Chippewa Nation settled along the river. It was there, around 1811, that a fur trader from Quebec, Jacob Smith, whose family lived in Detroit, established a trading post and became friends with Chief Neome. When the Saginaw Treaty of 1819 was signed, part of the treaty granted Smith's family and friends eleven tracts of land along the Flint River under their Chippewa names. Smith himself was adopted by the Chippewa and given the name *Wahbesins*, meaning "young swan." In the 1830s, the Native population was decimated by outbreaks of cholera and smallpox, diseases introduced by the White man.

The first permanent settlers were John and Polly Todd from Pontiac. In 1830, John Todd purchased lot no. 7 for $800 from Nowokeshik, a mixed-race employee of Smith whose European name was François Edouard Campau. The Todds established a tavern where downtown Flint is today. The first wedding in Flint was held there in 1831. A large dugout canoe was used by Todd and travelers to cross the Flint River, so the spot became known as Todd's Ferry. In 1834, the first bridge was built to span the river on the Saginaw Trail. The trail was upgraded to a turnpike by the following year. The white pine forest attracted lumbering interests, and the area developed into the Flint River Village. By 1854, seven lumber mills were operating, and Flint became a city in 1855.

By 1876, the supply of lumber was exhausted, and Flint became more of a farming community. But another industry was starting to take shape. Wagon maker William A. Paterson moved to Flint in 1869 and opened a carriage repair shop, which evolved into a carriage factory that became very successful and one of three major horse-drawn carriage factories in Flint. The others were the Flint Wagon Works and the Durant-Dort Carriage company, the largest of the three. Flint became known as the Vehicle City because of the carriage industry.

As motorized vehicles were coming into being, the carriage companies entered the motor vehicle marketplace as Flint Motor Works's James H. Whiting bought the failing Buick Motor Company and moved it to Flint. William C. "Billy" Durant of the Durant-Dort Carriage Company took over Buick, and his salesmanship made Buick automobiles successful. Carriage makers Paterson, as well as Durant-Dort partner J. Dallas Dort, also entered the automotive market in Flint.

Durant founded General Motors (GM) in 1908, with Buick as a subsidiary. The Durant-Dort Carriage Company's office building on Water Street is considered to be the birthplace of GM. Durant went on a buying spree acquiring other automotive companies and became overextended and lost control of GM in 1910. Durant then founded Chevrolet in 1911, using the old Flint Wagon Works location, and its success allowed Durant to take over GM again in 1916. But he lost control of GM for the final time in 1920, during an economic downturn. Flint's amazing growth in the early part of the twentieth century can be attributed to Durant. Sadly, Durant's final major venture, Durant Motors, went bankrupt during the Great Depression, and he became a footnote in automotive history.

As Flint had only one major industry—automotive—its fortunes were tied to that of the industry. Flint was hard hit by the Great Depression, but World War II, with the conversion of Flint's factories for the nation's war effort, led to additional GM factory construction. And at the end of the war, the city enjoyed great prosperity, which lasted into the mid twentieth century. The city of Flint's population peaked at nearly 200,000 in 1960.

LOST TO PROGRESS

As Flint grew, notable buildings and neighborhoods had to give way to benefit the city's growth.

Music Hall and Bijou Theatre

Flint's first theater was on the top floor of the three-story Fenton Building at the corner of Saginaw and Kearsley Streets, where the Kresge Building was later built and is now a parking lot. Called Fenton Hall and opened in 1866, it proved inadequate to stage grander productions, so in 1883, the first fully equipped theater was built.

Called the Music Hall, it was located at the corner of Harrison and First Streets. With 1,200 seats, it was Flint's only good auditorium for several years. It presented not only plays and musical performances but also school and civic gatherings. But the management ran into financial problems, so around 1894, businessman Oren Stone acquired it, and it was renamed Stone's Opera House. Later on, it included vaudeville shows, which were live variety shows in which itinerant performers traveled around the country to provide family entertainment to towns large and small. In 1913, the Stone family leased the theater to Colonel Walter S. Butterfield, who renamed the venue the Majestic Theatre and, after renovations, offered vaudeville full time. As larger and grander theaters were built, the Majestic presented roadshow acts, until it closed in 1921. It was torn down in 1923 to make room for the *Flint Journal*'s new home, and that now houses Michigan State University's College of Human Medicine.

Colonel Butterfield, who operated a chain of theaters in Michigan, opened Flint's first exclusive vaudeville theater, the Bijou Theatre, in 1905. He renovated a building with two storefronts into a simple theater with a small stage. The theater was remodeled in 1909, 1910 and 1913 and featured such acts as Marilyn Miller, the Marx Brothers, the Two Black Crows, Harry Langdon and Chic Sales. In 1915, the theater was remodeled again and renamed the Garden, switching to offering motion pictures exclusively. In 1929, the silent movie venue was converted to offer talkies with Vitaphone and Movietone sound.

By 1939, it was determined that despite the numerous remodels over the years, the converted theater had lost its step with the fast-moving film industry and came to be regarded as a relic. So, the old theater was torn

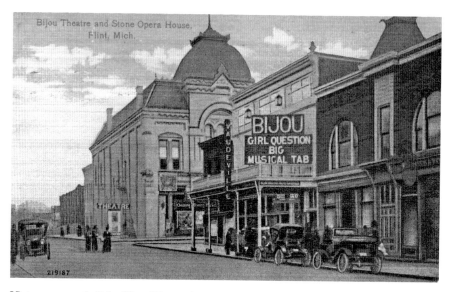

Vintage postcard of the Bijou Theatre in the foreground and Stone's Opera House (also known as Music Hall and Majestic Theatre) in the background. *Author's collection.*

down in April and May 1939, to be replaced by a new state-of-the-art Garden Theatre. With the rise of television in the 1950s, the Garden tried to keep pace by offering critically acclaimed films beginning on September 1, 1955, with *Marty*, which would win four Oscars. Alas, that policy did not pan out, so after the final showing of the 1954 biblical drama *Day of Triumph*, the Garden closed indefinitely on December 10, 1955. The Garden reopened on July 3, 1957, with an exclusive engagement of Cecil B. DeMille's *The Ten Commandments*. When the Capitol Theatre closed in 1957 to be modernized (which was reversed with the 2017 restoration), the Garden presented films that the Capitol would normally offer. Just before the Capitol Theatre reopened on Christmas Day 1957, the Garden offered a free show sponsored by local businesses that offered tickets to the western movie *Tomahawk Trail*, starring Chuck Connors with short subjects. Afterward, the Garden closed permanently. It was torn down in 1966 to make way for Genesee Towers, and an urban plaza is on the site today.

Oak Grove Hospital

Dr. C.R. Burr, medical director of the Oak Grove Hospital for most of its existence, began his 1930 memoir with the following: "It has been the fate of many of Earth's beauty spots to be devastated in the march of 'progress.' Such a calamity was narrowly averted at Oak Grove. A hospital for nervous and mental diseases under this name established in Flint in 1891 was located in a grove of majestic oaks which had been spared the woodman's axe through the foresight and benevolence of Governor [Henry H.] Crapo."

The local lumber baron who was elected Michigan governor had planned to build a mansion on the sixty-acre site, but it was never built. His estate sold the Oak Grove land for construction of the hospital, with Crapo's son William W. Crapo serving on the hospital's board of directors. The first medical director was Dr. George C. Palmer, who served until his death in 1894 and was succeeded by Dr. Burr, who served as medical director until the hospital closed in 1920.

The hospital consisted of several buildings connected by semicircular enclosed community corridors. The administration building was flanked on either side by buildings serving male patients on one side and female patients on the other. In 1895, Dr. James Noyes turned in his stock in the hospital to pay for a recreational building named Noyes Hall. It contained billiard rooms, an assembly hall, a bowling alley, an electrical room and hydro-therapeutic rooms.

At the time the hospital was built, Flint had a population of around ten thousand people. But by 1910, the city had quadrupled in number and

Oak Grove Sanitarium. *Author's collection.*

would more than double in population between 1910 and 1920. In 1919, the board of directors sold the hospital and its grounds to the Flint Board of Education for construction of a new high school. Flint Central High School was completed in 1922. The administrators of the hospital had plans to build a new hospital farther away from the city, but the post–World War I economy led to the abandonment of plans to build a new hospital. The Oak Grove Hospital announced it would close on April 28, 1920, the expiration of its corporate life. The staff was assembled at Noyes Hall the following June at the request of Dr. Burr, who made a surprise announcement that they would get additional compensation totaling $60,000, ranging from $160 to $4,800 based on their years of service.

The Flint Board of Education made use of the buildings, which were dubbed the Oak Grove Campus. Dr. Burr stated in 1930, "Much of the grove has been preserved. The original buildings are utilized as a teacher's club, for offices, for a museum, and for a school clinic. As for the high school itself, it is probable that none in this country has a handsomer setting."

It served as the home of Flint Junior College (now Mott Community College) until the present campus opened in 1955. In 1953, the former Noyes Hall was renovated to become home for the Flint Board of Education's new FM radio station, WFBE.

With the development of the Flint Cultural Center around the Oak Grove Campus buildings, demolition of the Oak Grove buildings began one by one, starting with the old men's department building, which was torn down for the new cafeteria/WFBE addition. The Central High cafeteria was on the upper level and the WFBE studios, transmitter and offices were on the lower. The former Noyes Hall was the final Oak Grove building torn down when WFBE moved to its new facilities in 1961. The former site became a parking lot serving both the high school and the Flint Institute of Arts. One building remains standing, the former carriage house behind Whittier Junior High School.

The Carnegie Public Library

The Flint Public Library dates to 1851, when the Ladies Library Association was founded with Maria Smith Stockton, daughter of Flint founder Jacob Smith, as its first president. In 1884, it evolved into the Flint Public Library, operated by the Board of the Union School District of Flint, which was the forerunner of the Flint Board of Education. In 1904, it moved into the first

Flint Public Library donated by Andrew Carnegie. *Author's collection.*

building designed as a library in Flint at the northeast corner of Kearsley and Clifford Streets, one of over 1,600 public libraries funded by steel magnate Andrew Carnegie.

But as Flint grew over the decades, the Carnegie library became too small for the Flint Public Library's growing collection. With the development of the College and Cultural Center in the 1950s, the Flint Public Library's main location moved to a much larger facility in the new Flint Cultural Center in 1958. The old Carnegie library was mainly vacant for the next two years, but in 1960, it briefly served as the local Democratic Party headquarters, until the old library building was dismantled later in 1960 or early 1961. The 1961 Polk directory indicated that this library's address at 301 East Kearsley Street ceased to exist. Today, that site is at the heart of the University of Michigan–Flint's downtown campus.

Quinn Chapel AME Church on East Seventh Street

The Quinn Chapel African Methodist Episcopal Church, the oldest Black congregation in Flint, was organized on Mill Street in 1875 at the home of Nancy West, under the supervision of Reverend John Furgeson. Paying for the construction of the first church building, built by churchmen at 121

East Seventh Street, was a long and severe struggle. Two young members employed at the Crapo Lumber Mill were talking to employer William Crapo, and Crapo donated enough lumber to build the church. For a time, the young men of the congregation held a debating society and charged a small admittance fee that went toward paying the church debt. The first church was dedicated in 1877. A small addition to the church was added to the rear in 1897 to give the choir more space.

Growing pains led to the original church's demolition in 1912 to make way for a larger brick church built on the site. A parsonage was added nearby at 1327 Liberty Street at the former home of church cofounder Nancy West, who bequeathed her home to the church in her will. A pipe organ was installed at the church in 1924. In the 1930s, an annex was constructed and new pews were installed. In 1939, choir members donated a baby grand piano to the church. In 1941, the organ was upgraded to include chimes.

Quinn Chapel AME Church served as an anchor to the Floral Park neighborhood south of downtown, where many Black Flintites lived in the era of segregation. But in 1955, Flint's city officials decided that the municipal services needed to be consolidated into a single campus. So, the city bought the church and demolished it that year. While the new church

Quinn Chapel AME Church on Seventh Street. *Flint Public Library.*

location on Lippincott Boulevard was being built, services were held in the former Mount Olive Baptist Church, which the congregation rented. The church was built in phases, and the congregation moved into the first portion on Lippincott in 1957. The completed church was dedicated in 1961.

Flint City Hall on Saginaw and Third Streets

In 1907, Flint voters approved construction of a new two-story city hall with a basement constructed of reinforced concrete with cut stone and brick and a fireproof tile roof. It replaced Flint's original city hall.

Located at the corner of Saginaw and Third Streets, it was completed in 1909. It served the city for almost fifty years. There was a fire at that city hall in 1938, but eleven fire rigs saved the building, which mostly suffered smoke and water damage.

It was torn down after the Flint Municipal Center was completed in 1958. Today, the McCree Courts and Human Services Center occupies the site that was built in 1965 as a Montgomery Ward department store.

City Hall on South Saginaw and Third Streets. *Author's collection.*

YMCA on Kearsley Street

While the Young Men's Christian Association, better known as the YMCA or casually referred to as the Y, was founded in London, England, in 1844 and spread to the United States in the 1850s, the YMCA's Flint activities date to 1879, when some interested citizens began Y programs. In 1913, Charles Stewart Mott was elected the first YMCA of Flint board president, and on December 13, the four-story building at the corner of Kearsley and Clifford (now Wallenberg) Streets first opened. Mott served as the Y's president until 1933.

This was the Y's location until January 21, 1962, when the present downtown YMCA officially opened at 411 East Third Street, taking up the whole block, which includes Stevens and East Second Streets as well as Chavez Drive, the southbound I-475 service drive.

On October 24, 1965, the Flint City Commission awarded the contract to demolish the former YMCA to make way for a surface parking lot. Today, the site is part of the University of Michigan–Flint parking ramp on Kearsley Street between Wallenberg and Harrison Streets.

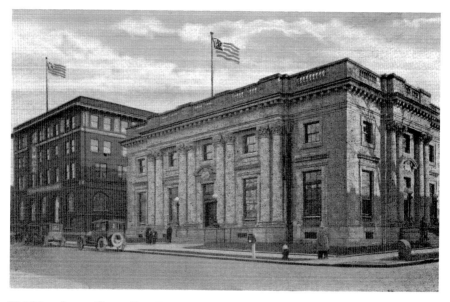

YMCA and post office on East Kearsley Street. *Author's collection.*

Post Office/Community Service Center

The year is 1905, which was the city of Flint's Golden Jubilee. On June 7, a parade was held featuring Vice President Charles W. Fairbanks. That same day, a cornerstone was laid for a new Federal Building and post office, which was completed two years later at the southeast corner of Kearsley and Harrison Streets. That post office was controversial at that time, because many people considered it to be too small in relation to the mail volume. That proved to be true, for in 1931, the post office moved to a much larger facility at 600 Church Street, which then became the Federal Building and United States District Court after the main post office moved to its present location off Robert T. Longway Boulevard around 1960.

After the post office moved out of its original location, the building stood vacant at times. It became the local headquarters for the Works Progress Administration, a Depression-era New Deal agency. After it left, the National Youth Administration moved in. It stood vacant again after that organization left. The Junior Chamber of Commerce used it briefly as a depot for sending clothing abroad.

In 1944, Charles Stewart Mott bought the white elephant from the federal government for $17,500. It needed a lot of work. In 1948, the War Chest of Flint, which was a World War II–era relief organization, dissolved itself and donated the surplus funds for the repair and renovation of the old post office. Contractors charged just 55 percent of what construction would normally cost for renovating what became known as the Community Service Center. It housed various agencies funded by the Community Chest (later Red Feather Fund), which is now known as the United Way. It was dedicated on September 28, 1948.

But in 1966, the Community Service Center was torn down to make way for a parking ramp and a downtown branch of the Flint Public Library. Taken over by the University of Michigan–Flint, it is still used as a parking ramp by the university, with the former library space now occupied by UM–Flint's Engineering Design Studio and Learning Space.

Savoy/Rialto/Royal Theatre

With the growing popularity of television in the 1950s, like with other large cities, most movie theaters located downtown or in neighborhoods closed one by one. One theater that managed to survive into the 1970s in downtown Flint was known for most of its existence as the Rialto Theatre.

It was built in 1909 as the Savoy Theatre by former entertainer Louis Sunlin and offered both live vaudeville acts and movies. After Sunlin died in 1935 at age eighty, the theater was sold, remodeled and renamed the Rialto. While the Rialto offered movies, it also had vaudeville acts on Saturdays, Sundays and Mondays under manager Maxie Gealer, who led his own act, Maxie & the Gang, on vaudeville nights, as well as presenting guest performers, such as the Three Stooges, who appeared at the Rialto in 1938. The theater offered all-night movies for the benefit of factory workers.

In 1961, the theater changed its name to the Royal and offered art and foreign films, which were not well received in the blue-collar town. Four years later, it was leased to Nathan J. Schwartz, who offered a different mix of movies for adults only, which were initially grindhouse films and evolved into softcore then hardcore pornography.

In 1973, Citizens Bank bought the entire block of South Saginaw Street to Union Street north of the bank building for a planned new office tower. The Royal was torn down, but the 1973 Arab Oil Embargo and the resulting recession delayed construction of that tower until 1977. Completed in 1978, successor bank First Merit sold it to the University of Michigan in 2015, expanding the downtown campus even farther downtown. It is now the University Tower Building.

LOST TO DISASTERS

Hotel Dresden

The Hotel Dresden was opened on January 30, 1907, by carriage maker, auto builder and real estate developer William A. Paterson. Located at 700 South Saginaw Street at the corner of Saginaw and Third Streets, it was named after Dresden, Germany, by Paterson's daughter Mary, who was impressed when she visited. At the time of its opening, it had 103 guest chambers. The six-story building was considered Flint's finest hotel until the rival Durant Hotel was built in 1920.

Hotel Dresden, later known as the Milner and then Adams Hotel. *Author's collection.*

Adams Hotel after it was destroyed by fire in 1963. *Courtesy of Kenneth Sherman.*

The hotel changed ownership a number of times over the years, and in 1940, it was acquired by the Detroit-based Milner Hotels chain and renamed the Milner. A 1954 fire at the Milner gutted two basement rooms. The following year, the hotel was considered a fire trap, so repairs were made. In 1959, attorney B. Morris Pelavin bought the hotel and renamed it the Adams. He also established his law office there. Pelavin extensively remodeled the interior and removed all possible fire hazards. On August 11, 1963, the 116-room hotel was destroyed in a spectacular fire that claimed three lives and was blamed on careless smoking. Most of the 109 registered guests were asleep at that time. The Flint Fire Department made several daring rescues and was assisted by staff, including the hotel manager and an elevator operator.

Pelavin built a new office building one block south of where the hotel stood, appropriately called the Phoenix Building. An addition to the First Presbyterian Church was built where the hotel once stood.

The J. Dallas Dort Home

In 1906, J. Dallas Dort, who co-owned the Durant-Dort Carriage Company (with William C. Durant), moved with his family into a large, stately home at the corner of Kearsley and Crapo Streets. Dort played the cello, and the home was fitted with an Aeolian pipe organ that he liked to play for guests. Dort founded the Choral Union in 1913 and in 1917 founded the forerunner of the Flint Institute of Music.

Dort died of a heart attack in 1925. His widow, Marcia, continued to live in the home until she turned it over to the Cultural Center for use as a music school in 1958. It was named the Dort Music Building.

The Dort family contributed greatly to the facility's expansion, but in 1970, during construction of the expanded Dort Music Center, which would have used the old Dort home, it was destroyed by fire. Many of the surviving pages of sheet music had to be laid out individually to dry before mildew could set in.

The Dort Music Center, housing the Flint Institute of Music and the Flint Symphony Orchestra, was completed in 1971. Expanded and renovated in 2005, it is a lasting legacy to the Dort family's contribution to the arts.

J. Dallas Dort home, which became the Dort Music Building. *Flint Public Library.*

Lost to Neglect

Paterson Factory One/Pengelly Building

One significant building in downtown Flint was built in the 1880s or '90s as a three-and-a-half-story factory with a four-story addition attached at the corner of Third and Harrison Streets by the W.A. Paterson Company, which was a major manufacturer of horse-drawn carriages and later built automobiles. The company folded in 1923, two years after Paterson's death. Paterson Factory no. 1 was sold in 1928 to J. Bradford Pengelly, the former rector of St. Paul's Episcopal Church, who chose a new career in real estate. Renamed the Pengelly Building, it was converted into an office building with storefronts on the ground floor. It housed mostly labor unions and was the base of operations for organizing the 1936–37 Flint sit-down strike. But Pengelly lost ownership of the building in 1932 in a mortgage foreclosure. It went through three different owners over the next few years.

Even during the sit-down strike, the aging building was considered to be a rickety firetrap. A water tank on the building's roof was a source of complaints until it collapsed three stories into the basement due to the excess weight. It took several months to clear the debris and repair damage to offices and stores.

The Pengelly Building was vacated due to renovation plans with the Flint Federation of Labor and the Flint and Genesee Building Trades Council moving into the former Industrial Savings Bank Building, which was renamed the CIO Building. The CIO Building is now part of Northbank Center. But after the 1941 Pearl Harbor attack and America's entry into World War II, the federal government rejected plans to rehabilitate the Pengelly Building. Dilapidated and boarded up, it was sold to Hamady Bros. Food Markets in 1946 and torn down. Due to postwar material shortages, the site became a parking lot.

A Hamady Bros. Food Market was finally built on the site in 1954. Later used as a Skaff Furniture store, the building now houses the Ennis Center for Children.

Lakeside Park and Flint Park

In the 1920s and 1930s, Flint had two amusement parks that were adjacent to lakes. The first to open was Lakeside Park, along Thread Lake at the corner of Orville Street and Peer Avenue, and the second was Flint Park at the corner of Dupont Street and Stewart Avenue.

Lakeside Park opened on May 30, 1913. It boasted the longest roller coaster in Michigan at that time when it opened in 1916. It featured live entertainment, a baseball field, a dance hall, various rides, concession stands and canoeing on Thread Lake, among other attractions. The ongoing effects of the Great Depression, along with competition from Flint Park across town, led to it close permanently after the 1931 season. The park was sold to the city of Flint by the estate of D.D. Aitken in 1936 for $20,000. The city demolished the amusement park structures, and it was absorbed into the city's adjacent Thread Lake Park. The combined park was renamed McKinley Park on July 4, 1942, in memory of George E. McKinley, who served as Flint mayor and was a longtime parks administrator.

Flint Park opened on May 30, 1921. Admission was free until the streetcar line was extended to serve the park by July 4 of that year. Developed on nearly forty acres of Matthew Davison's farm, it had the usual amusements park rides, including a roller coaster, plus dancing, circus acts and balloon rides. Devil's Lake on the site was renamed Flint Park Lake. Over the nearly forty years the park was in operation, it added attractions from season to season.

Lakeside Park. *Courtesy of Mary Wade Wright.*

A Movie Drome and a baseball diamond were among the new attractions by 1924. Along with additional rides, the 1931 season added shuffleboard, archery, croquet, boating and horseshoes. Fourth of July fireworks were held annually. Louis Armstrong performed on July 1, 1933. President Harry S. Truman campaigned there in 1948. But by the late 1950s, the nature of the park's clientele was changing. The crowd was getting rough, and vandalism was becoming a problem. On the park's final day, Labor Day 1960, a fare-thee-well fireworks display was held.

On March 31, 1961, Flint Park management announced it was closed permanently and the site would be redeveloped. Demolition had already begun, and a shopping center was developed along Dupont Street in 1964. The rest of the former Flint Park site was neglected, and Flint Park Lake became unsafe to swim in. Eventually, the remaining twenty acres were redeveloped by the city as Flint Park Lake park.

Walter Winchester Hospital

In 1927, Genesee County built the Genesee County Infirmary at 4562 Flushing Road in Flint Township to provide medical services to welfare patients. In 1941, Dr. Walter H. Winchester, who at the time was medical director of the Genesee County Welfare Department, was appointed medical superintendent of the infirmary until he retired in 1962. In 1961, it was renamed Walter Winchester Hospital in his honor. He died in 1963 at age eighty-eight after serving as a physician in the area since 1910. At age eighty, he was honored by the Michigan State Medical Society as "foremost physician of the year."

In 1967, administrative functions were consolidated with the county's Genesee Memorial Hospital at 702 South Ballenger Highway. In 1969, state aid for Winchester was reduced by $3,000 a day. This led to cost cutting, which was not enough for the hospital. It lost its status as a hospital that year and was renamed the Walter Winchester Unit of Genesee Memorial Hospital.

But in 1970, Winchester closed. In 1972, medical equipment and furnishings were auctioned off and the former hospital was converted to offices for the Genesee County Department of Social Services. After the county moved out in 1983, businessman and future Flint mayor Don Williamson bought the former hospital in 1990. Considered to be haunted, it became a target for vagrants and vandals by 1997. The following year,

Williamson sold the property to New Calvary Cemetery, and the old hospital was torn down shortly afterward. The plans are to eventually develop an annex for the cemetery.

Lost Neighborhoods to "Progress"

With the construction of expressways and 1960s urban renewal projects, two neighborhoods can be considered lost. Parts of one neighborhood date to before Flint was a city. The second neighborhood developed with the construction of Buick factories on Flint's north side. Because of racial discrimination and restrictive covenants in force before the 1960s, these two neighborhoods became largely Black communities.

Floral Park

Floral Park is officially the name of a subdivision that was platted in 1909 along Floral Park Avenue on the south part of the neighborhood. This subdivision is still intact. But the northern part was wiped out in two stages. The first stage came in the Flint centennial year of 1955, when the Flint Municipal Center was developed as a single campus, including city hall, police department and fire department. The Flint Municipal Center campus was dedicated in 1958. The second stage came with the clearance of land that was in the path of the I-475 and M-78 (later I-69) expressways, including the interchange for both expressways wiping out the north side of the neighborhood in 1968. Parts of the northern section of the neighborhood date back to when Flint was a village, before it was incorporated as a city in 1855. It developed into a thriving predominately Black neighborhood convenient to downtown with an active social life. The Golden Leaf Club, which is still in operation, became a thriving nightclub, known for its live music.

St. John Street

With the construction of what would become the Buick factory complex in 1906 on the site of the Hamilton Farm, there were new residential

A 1968 advertisement for People's Furniture & Appliance emergency sale, which was forced to move due to expressway development. *Flint Public Library.*

and commercial developments east of the complex and east of the Pere Marquette (later CSX) rail line. Beginning with the Fairview subdivision platted in 1907, continuing with the Buick Heights and General Motors Park Number One subdivisions in 1909 and an addition to General Motors Park in 1916, a neighborhood anchored by St. John Street developed. With the influx of new residents employed by Buick and its nearby suppliers, this neighborhood developed into a "little Europe" because of the large number of immigrants employed in Flint factories. Up to thirty-four countries were represented in the neighborhood.

Over time, as the new residents adjusted to life, their children were Americanized and the families could afford better housing elsewhere, the ethnic makeup of the neighborhood gradually changed. In 1940, the racial makeup was 60 percent White, primarily Catholics from southern and eastern Europe. In the 1950s, Black people made up the majority of the population. Because of the pollution from the adjacent Buick complex, it was less desirable compared to the cleaner Floral Park area, so it became home to Flint's economically disadvantaged Black residents. The neighborhood became a haven for crime and vice.

When Interstate 475 was in the planning stages in the 1960s, General Motors was looking for an easy way to get bodies, assembled at the Fisher Body no. 1 plant on Flint's south side, transported to the Buick final assembly plant on Flint's north side, adjacent to the St. John Street neighborhood. So, that was how I-475 was routed. It cut into the St. John Street neighborhood and isolated much of the east side of the neighborhood, except for an overpass on Massachusetts Avenue.

The fate of the neighborhood was sealed with planning for the St. John Industrial Park as an urban renewal project in the late 1960s, but funding problems delayed land acquisition for a decade, allowing the neighborhood to deteriorate further. Property acquisition was finally completed in 1977, allowing for the demolition of nearly all of the buildings in the St. John Street neighborhood to create the St. John Industrial Park, which included expansion of the Buick manufacturing complex, dubbed Buick City. In the process, Buick switched to unibody construction, which eliminated the need for the Fisher Body no. 1 plant on the south side. St. John Street was rerouted and became an extension of James P. Cole Boulevard. Some parts of the old St. John Street still remain, including the portion intersecting Massachusetts Avenue, where the former police academy (previously a community center) is still standing but abandoned.

The Original Doyle Neighborhood

Named for Doyle School, built in 1902, which continues to anchor the neighborhood, the Doyle Neighborhood boundaries are Saginaw Street to the west, Cornelia Street to the north, Industrial Avenue to the east and Fifth Avenue to the south. The street running north-south through the neighborhood was North Street. Three streets ran east-west, McFarlan, Margaret and Louisa Streets.

The oldest part of the neighborhood was part of the Village of Grand Traverse, which was platted in 1837 and developed by Chauncey Payne, son-in-law of Flint founder Jacob Smith. The village's northernmost street on the plat map was later renamed Margaret Street. The portion north of the Village of Grand Traverse plat map was later developed in two stages by local lumber mill owner and former Flint mayor Alexander McFarlan, who developed several subdivisions in early Flint history. The neighborhood portion south of McFarlan Street was named McFarlan & Company's Saginaw Street addition in 1871, and the portion north of McFarlan Street became part of McFarlan & Company's Northern Addition in 1872.

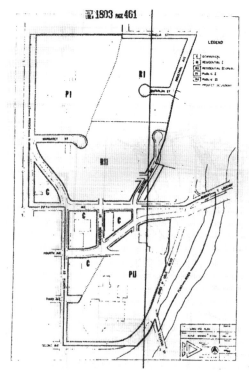

Left: The planned Doyle urban renewal development from 1971. *Flint Public Library.*

Opposite: The neighborhood north of downtown that was wiped out by the Doyle urban renewal development. *Flint Public Library.*

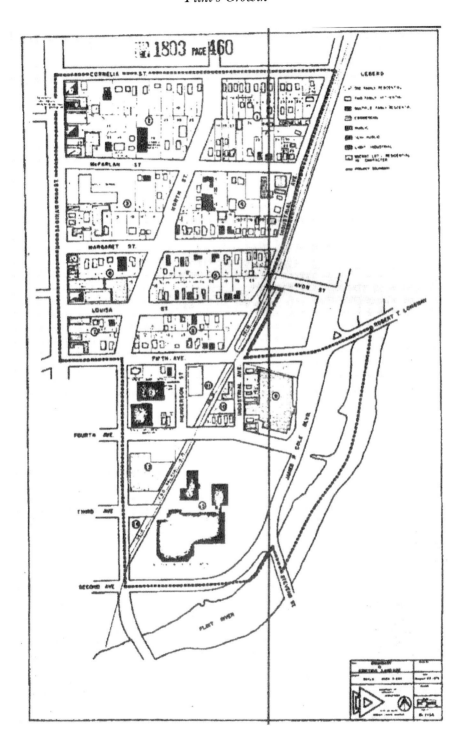

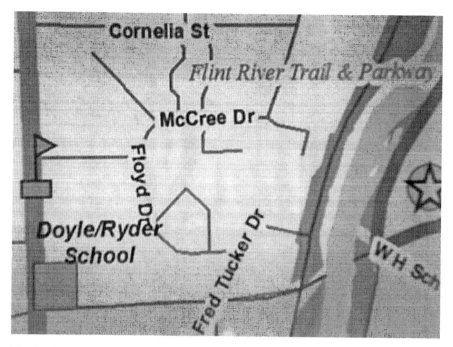

The Doyle urban renewal neighborhood that developed. *City of Flint.*

As the commercial part of the neighborhood along North Saginaw Street developed, two movie theaters were built, the Regent in 1919 at 906 North Saginaw and the Ritz in 1920 at 1200 North Saginaw. When television came along, the Ritz was renovated into the Flint Arcade office building in 1952. The Regent became a church in the 1960s. By the 1960s, much of the residential housing in the neighborhood became substandard and was considered to be slum housing.

In 1971, the Doyle Urban Renewal plan was unveiled. It was a complete makeover of the neighborhood, which wiped out every structure outside of historic Doyle School. The school was rehabilitated and became Doyle-Ryder School. All of the streets in the area were replaced by culs-de-sac.

The name given to the new neighborhood was River Village, which consisted of three residential developments, the high-rise River Village Senior Apartments, the three-story Gardenview Apartments and the Schafer Square Apartments, which were townhouses. The commercial development was Windmill Place, which was ultimately unsuccessful and is mentioned in detail later in this book.

THE WHITE FLIGHT TO THE SUBURBS

Flint's population peaked at 196,940 in 1960. The 1970 population fell to 193,317. Genesee County's population grew from 374,313 in 1960 to 444,341 in 1970. Expressway development and urban renewal projects forced the relocation of Floral Park and St. John Street neighborhood residents. When this happened, restrictive covenants on deeds, along with homeowners who didn't want to live in integrated neighborhoods and real estate agents who steered home buyers into certain neighborhoods, Black home buyers were kept from moving into more desirable neighborhoods.

The lack of housing opportunities led to protests and unrest in the late 1960s. Civil unrest on July 24 and 25, 1967, in the wake of the Detroit riots, affected the St. John Street and Floral Park neighborhoods, as well as Flint's north side. Curfews and restrictions on sale of alcohol, gasoline and guns were imposed in the wake of the disturbances. WAMM AM 1420 (now WFLT) radio, which was a daytime-only station at that time, was allowed to stay on the air during the unrest. The disturbances led to calls the following month for more employment opportunities for Black youths and for open housing and equal accommodations. But the Flint City Commission voted down a fair housing ordinance the following month. That led to ten days of protests attracting four thousand people. Residents held a sleep-in in front of city hall, and Governor George Romney showed up at a unity rally. Two months later, the commission reversed itself and approved the ordinance. But opponents signed petitions forcing a vote. On February 20, 1968, voters approved the fair housing ordinance by a very narrow forty-three-vote margin out of more than forty thousand votes cast.

The Federal Fair Housing Act of 1968 made restrictive covenants illegal and unenforceable and prohibited discrimination based on race, religion or place of national origin. Governor Romney also signed a tough Michigan open housing bill. Despite legislation on the local, state and national levels, segregation based on housing patterns continued.

As Black families moved out of the St. John Street and Floral Park neighborhoods in the wake of I-475 construction and urban renewal projects, some local real estate agents began conducting either door-to-door or by-phone offers to White homeowners in much of the city, which affected Flint's north and northwest sides west of the Buick complex, as well as on the southeast side adjacent to Floral Park. That had some residents accusing real estate agents of illegal blockbusting, the practice of pressuring homeowners to sell because the ethnic makeup of the neighborhood was changing. White homeowners would sell their houses below market value to real estate companies that would then sell the homes to Black buyers at a considerable profit. By 1973, the proliferation of for sale signs on front lawns led for calls to restrict the placement of signage. While the Flint Board of Realtors opposed this, it did favor certain restrictions, such as restricting placement of commercial for sale signs and prohibiting telephone and door-to-door solicitations by real estate agents looking for homes for sale.

But that did not stem the White flight from the north and northwest sides and part of the southeast side between I-69 and Lippincott Boulevard. Between 1970 and 1980, the White population declined from 138,065 to 89,470, while the Black population increased from 54,237 to 66,164. In 1990, the White population decreased to 69,788, and the Black population increased to 67,485. In the 2000 census, Flint shifted to a Black majority, with 66,560 Black and 51,710 White residents living in the city of Flint.

Part II

FLINT'S DECLINE

Lost to the University of Michigan–Flint Downtown Campus

On March 1972, plans were announced to move the growing University of Michigan–Flint from the Mott Memorial Building adjacent to the Genesee (now Mott) Community College campus on East Court Street to downtown Flint in an area bounded by Kearsley, Stevens and Harrison Streets and the Flint River. Much of the area was city owned and used for parking. But the site included the locations of the Taystee Bread bakery and the Palace Theatre, as well as the Grand Trunk Western Railroad.

One month later, in April 1972, the former YWCA, in use from 1925 to 1968, reopened after renovations. It became Bridal Village, a collection of related wedding shops. It contained Nancy Carol's Bridals, the Printshop, Maxine's Cakery, Lloyd Thompson's Flowers, Village Jewelers, H&D Tuxedo, Samsrume Boutique and Bertrum Elliott Photography. A beauty shop, dance hall and reception room were completed by June.

The university had plans to develop a campus at the corner of Court Street and Lapeer Road and built the Surge Building to accommodate overflow from the Mott Memorial Building. The following July, the city purchased the American Bakeries Taystee bread plant, allowing the bakery to continue operating for up to eighteen months.

The future location of the University of Michigan–Flint campus in the 1950s, with the Palace Theatre in the bottom center. *Author's collection.*

But by the start of 1974, the downtown campus boundaries expanded southward to East First Street and eastward to the I-475 right of way. The first move in expanding the campus was turning over Willson Park from the city to the university, though it continued as a park. The city OK'd the razing of the Taystee Bread bakery on Stevens Street and the Texaco station on East Kearsley Street. The bakery, built in 1889 as the J.B. Armstrong Manufacturing Company, was demolished in March 1974. The factory made springs and axles for the carriage and later auto industry, until it was absorbed into General Motors. It was converted into a bakery in 1909, when Greissell Baking Company moved there. Horse-drawn wagons were originally used for deliveries, so there was a large sign saying WAGON-ROOM cut into stone blocks above an entrance. That sign was saved and is now on display inside historic Factory One on Water Street. American Bakeries, the baker of Taystee Bread, bought the bakery in 1953.

The official groundbreaking for the new campus took place on May 9, 1974. The following November, the university began moving into the campus site after taking over the Brooks and Penfield apartment buildings at the corner of Kearsley and Stevens Streets. The apartments were converted into offices to free space in the Mott Memorial Building for additional classrooms. There was no further space for temporary outdoor classrooms outside the eleven units in place around the building.

On December 1974, the city began condemnation proceedings on Nancy Carol's Bridal Village in the old YWCA. Nancy Carol (whose real name was Nancy Adado) and her husband Sam refused the city's $320,000 offer to buy the building.

On July 1975, condemnation proceedings began on the original location of Bill Thomas's Halo Burger; the former Kewpee Hamburgs, founded in 1923 at 417 Harrison Street; and the Palace Theatre built in 1917 at the corner of Kearsley and Harrison Streets. Despite pleas to save the theater for university use, it was torn down because it would cost at least $900,000 to renovate and bring it up to code. It closed on January 1976 and was torn down in February 1977. Other buildings were torn down to make way for the university, and the old YWCA gave way on November 1976. Halo Burger no. 1 gave way the following month, with the staff transferred to the new Halo Burger on Court Street near Center Road in Flint (which closed permanently in 2020). A historic two-story home at First and Stevens that was renovated into doctors' offices by dentist Dr. Kenneth Shelley was also lost.

The first university buildings—the Classroom Office Building (now French Hall) and the adjacent theater—were completed in 1977. The Harding Mott University Center was finished in 1979. That allowed the temporary offices, built around 1909 as the Brooks and Penfield apartment

The YWCA on First and Harrison Streets, later Bridal Village, which was razed to make way for the University of Michigan–Flint downtown campus. *Author's collection.*

buildings, to be torn down in 1980. The Murchie Science Building was constructed on that site. The final old building to be demolished for the campus was the King's Daughters & Sons home, which was built in 1931 and torn down fifty years later, in 1981. It was originally a childcare center before it was converted into a home for the aged, until it closed in 1975 to make way for the campus. It moved into a former hotel that was built as the Voyager Inn.

One structure that survives today is the parking ramp at the corner of Kearsley and Harrison Streets, which the university made use of for parking, as well as the former Flint Public Library inside the ramp, which is now the Engineering Design Studio & Learning Space. Also saved was the Hubbard Industrial Supply building. Hubbard Supply still operates from West Second Street and dates to 1865. The former Hubbard Supply Building at 602 Mill Street now houses the UM–Flint Department of Public Safety and is called the Hubbard Building.

LOST TO "PROGRESS"

The Riverbank Park Flood Control Project

The Flint River is prone to seasonal flooding, which still occurs in Flint parks. But serious flooding caused property damage in 1904, 1916, 1938, 1942 and especially 1947, which led to plans to control damage. The first project was the acquisition of land in 1950 along the Genesee and Lapeer County line near Columbiaville for the construction of the Holloway Dam, which created the Holloway Reservoir.

Next, the Army Corps of Engineers paved the Flint Riverbed from the Third Street (now University Avenue)/Sunset Drive bridge to where Swartz Creek branches off at the Grand Trunk Railway bridges (now the Genesee Valley Trail bridges using the old railroad bridge piers). It passes through the old "Chevy in the hole" manufacturing complex site, which, on the south side of the river, is now parkland called Chevy Commons. Kettering University claimed the north side of the river for campus expansion.

City officials held out for something more attractive in the downtown area rather than the stark concrete bed. To make way for what became Riverbank Park, the following buildings had to come down.

The portion of downtown Flint that was lost to Riverbank Park and the Hyatt Regency Hotel, with the Center Building below the Chevrolet billboard, which was built above the Flint River. *Author's collection.*

On North Saginaw Street, the most unusual of Flint's buildings was the Center Building at 201 North Saginaw, built *above* the Flint River circa 1925. Next to it was Moore Clothes at the corner of North Saginaw Street at First Avenue. Across the street was the Walsh Building, built circa 1910 at 310–320 North Saginaw.

On South Saginaw Street, Schiappassee Candy Kitchen was a Flint landmark dating to 1886 at 103 South Saginaw. But in February 1971, Albert Schiappassee reluctantly closed that candy store. He died the following June. Sharing that building dating to 1912 was Cowles & Co. At 107 South Saginaw, which began as a jewelry store and evolved into an optical office. The large neon eyeglasses suspended over the sidewalk were a local landmark. Across the street were Satan's Book Store and U.S. Coney Island.

Along East Water Street were the Silver Rail Bar and a Sears warehouse. West Water Street had the Famous Motor Lounge, Flint Vending Company, Addressograph Multigraph workshop, Flint Auto Glass, Wright Bros. Collision and Bill Carr Signs. First Avenue had Typewriter Exchange and an Eagles Hall.

Garland Street had Flint Business Machines, a barbershop and a cleaning business. Harrison Street had the Flint Home Furnishings warehouse.

By 1976, all of the structures mentioned were demolished. Plans for the beautification of the Riverbank Park flood control project were designed by Lawrence Halprin & Associates. It was completed in 1979 and dedicated with a free concert by Rick Nelson at the newly completed amphitheater.

Lost to the Hyatt Regency Hotel

In 1978, plans were announced for a Hyatt Regency Hotel along the downtown riverfront, which forced the closing of the last of the downtown Coney Island restaurants located near the Flint River, Flint Original Coney Island, part of downtown Flint since 1925. Another noted business was the Mad Hatter hat shop, which was forced to move. Another doomed building was the relocated Royal Theatre formerly in the aforementioned former Rialto Theatre, until it was torn down in 1973 to make way for a Citizens Bank tower.

Construction of the Hyatt also led to the loss of two notable historic buildings. One was the eight-story Commerce Building, built in 1925 to house Kobacker's Furniture. The Kobacker building was noted for its intricate brickwork. After the furniture store closed around 1949, it briefly housed a department store and then a men's clothing store, including the temporary location of A.M. Davison's while its store was rebuilt. The building was converted into an office building in 1955 by insurance man Ivan A. MacArthur and real estate agent Herbert E. Crouter. Called the MacArthur Building, it was sold to the Catsman Companies in 1965. It was then remodeled and renamed the Commerce Building. At that time, the first four floors were occupied by Michigan Bell Telephone Company, starting in 1959. The company moved out around 1968, and the main floor was vacant until around 1975, when the Citizens Bank credit card department moved in.

The other notable building was a four-story structure built by the Dort Motor Company in 1916 as a showroom for its vehicles at the corner of Water and Beach Streets. In 1923, that building was sold, and for the rest of its existence, it functioned as a furniture store. The freight elevator, which was large enough to haul cars, was suitable for moving large furniture. It was home to Winegarden's Furniture, until it closed in 1962. Other furniture stores took over the space, including United Home Outfitting, Bargain Benny's Supermarket Furniture and Chiplee's Supermarket Furniture. Pierce Furniture was the final business at that building. It was torn down along with the rest of the buildings in the Hyatt Regency's path in 1979.

Completed and opened in 1981, the sixteen-story Hyatt Regency was built for $30 million and boasted 369 rooms with a ballroom that can hold 1,200 people. A decade later, it was converted to a Radisson Hotel and then a Ramada Inn in 1999.

In 2000, a Christian organization called the Institute of Basic Life Principles, based in Illinois, bought the hotel and converted it into the Riverfront Character Inn. The management forbad drinking, smoking, rock music and adult movies. Housing its Verity University, it operated for five years. But then the Institute of Basic Life Principles put the hotel back on the market in 2005, and it was in limited use from that point onward.

There was an unsuccessful attempt in 2007 to buy the property for $9 million to use as privately owned housing for University of Michigan–Flint students. The Crim Fitness Foundation attempted to buy the former hotel as a fitness center, but the Institute of Basic Life Principles refused the Crim's offer as too low. Finally, in 2009, Uptown Reinvestment Corporation used a $27 million repayable grant from the Charles Stewart Mott Foundation to buy the vacant Riverfront Character Inn. Renamed the Riverfront Residence Hall, it was renovated into dormitories. In 2015, the Mott Foundation waved the grant, allowing Uptown Reinvestment to donate Riverfront Residence Hall to UM–Flint.

LOST TO WATER STREET PAVILION

In 1969 and 1970, two large regional shopping malls opened and siphoned shoppers from downtown Flint. The Eastland Mall (now Courtland Center) in what was then Burton Township (now the city of Burton) at the corner of Court Street and Center Road opened in 1969, and the Genesee Valley Shopping Center in Flint Township at the corner of Linden and Miller Roads opened in 1970. That immediately led to the closure of the downtown locations of F.W. Woolworth Company and Sears, Roebuck & Company, which both moved to Genesee Valley. While the other larger department stores in downtown Flint hung on for a few years, they closed in 1979 and 1980. J.C. Penney left downtown Flint at the end of 1979 and opened two new stores at the two aforementioned shopping malls.

Montgomery Ward and Smith-Bridgman's both closed in 1980. The number of vacant storefronts increased when businesses either moved or closed. That led to plans in 1983 by the Downtown Development Authority (DDA) and the Mott Foundation to develop a festival marketplace called Water Street Pavilion, which required the demolition of buildings covering two city blocks in the heart of downtown Flint, including several landmark and historic buildings.

Bryant House

Possibly the oldest structure razed to make way for Water Street Pavilion was what was left of the former Bryant House hotel, a four-story building that was built in the 1870s. In 1936, the top two stories were dismantled, and the first floor was converted into a series of storefronts. Upstairs, a curved stairway led to the ceiling. Tall arched windows were bricked in. A modern façade outside hid the changes. Leaning against the walls were a few doors with transom windows and room numbers still on the door panels. The final owner was Avery's Men's Wear, which occupied the north end of the building at South Saginaw at Union Street.

The Former Hubbard Hardware Complex

Hubbard Hardware was founded in 1865 by George W. Hubbard and partner H.B. Newton. Hubbard bought out his partner five years later. The four-story hardware store at 327 South Saginaw Street was built after a fire destroyed the three-story building that Hubbard occupied on that site in 1913. It evolved into a wholesale and retail operation with an overhead walkway above Brush Alley connecting to a large five-story warehouse that was later expanded to nine stories. An industrial supply division was also established. In 1963, the business was sold, and the new owners decided to close the retail and wholesale side of the business after ninety-eight years of operation. The industrial supply business, now called Hubbard Supply Company, is still in operation, with locations in Flint, Saginaw and Battle Creek. After Hubbard Hardware closed, J.C. Penney operated an annex store in the space where the catalog and toy departments were located from around 1965 to 1972. It has stood vacant since then.

Sill Building

The Sill Building was Flint's first skyscraper, built in 1911, and was called the Flint P. Smith Building. When it was completed, it consisted of 168 rooms for tenants. The lobby featured veined Italian marble. Smith was the son of lumberman Hiram "Hardwood" Smith. The younger Smith died during construction, and his widow completed it. She sold it to a stock company in 1915 for an estimated $150,000. It went through several owners over the years, and in 1949, it was renamed the Sill Building by Dr. Ervin Sill, a dentist and part owner. In 1965, it became a condominium. Each floor had a different owner, the first such commercial building sold this way in Michigan. It was managed by the Darby & Son real estate firm, which used the income to renovate the lobby and install air conditioners. The Flint Downtown Development Authority acquired the building in 1983 for $800,000, which led to its demolition.

Some of the buildings in downtown Flint that were lost to the Water Street Pavilion development. They included the Sill (Flint P. Smith) Building, Flint's first skyscraper. *Author's collection.*

Smith-Bridgman Building

Flint's heritage business was Smith, Bridgman and Company, founded in 1862 by William L. Smith. Employee Charles T. Bridgman became a partner in 1871 to create Smith-Bridgman. In 1923, the first of three seven-story sections was built at the site of the original location. A second addition with a similar façade was constructed in 1936, and the final addition on the south side, which replaced the ornate façade with a windowless modern one, was added in 1957. In 1970, it was sold to L.S. Good & Company of Wheeling, West Virginia. While it did open suburban Smith-Bridgman locations in Grand Blanc and Davison, the parent company filed for bankruptcy in 1979, and the downtown store closed for good in 1980. That store was the oldest department store in Michigan and one of four west of New York State that had operated at the same location for more than one hundred years.

Milner Arcade

The Milner Arcade, at the corner of South Saginaw and East First Street, was the most unusual in regard to its architecture. Dating to 1923, this three-story building was a hodgepodge of architectural styles, including Mediterranean, Tudor and Art Deco, facing First Street. Because of its small footprint at the corner location, there were calls to save this building. The DDA decided to hold off on demolition until it was determined to be sound enough to save. Alas, the Mott Foundation decided that the building was too far gone to be saved.

Kresge/Fenton Building

In 1923, the Fenton Block at the southeast corner of Saginaw and Kearsley Streets was torn down to make way for the four-story Kresge Building, which had offices on the upper floors and storefronts anchored by the S.S. Kresge Company variety store and lunch counter on the main floor. By the 1950s, it had taken over almost all of the main floor and basement. After Kresge closed that store in 1977, the owners of the building adopted the name of the building that it replaced, calling it the Fenton Building. The similar McCrory variety store took over the space but had to close due to the building's impending demise.

Former Home Dairy Building

The five-story Home Dairy Building was built in 1929 and originally housed the Home Dairy store, which sold groceries and had a soda fountain and restaurant. It was in business until 1964, when it lost its lease. It had plans to remodel but was unable to obtain a lease extension. In 1966, Smith-Bridgman opened a Store for the Home, offering appliances. It lasted about a decade. In 1978, Michael Rizik bought it to house businesses run by family members, including Michigan Bookkeeping, Income Tax Service Co., Business Analysis Co., Computer-Rizik Company and Johnny Fast-Print Co. The businesses operated for a couple of years, but by 1981, the building stood vacant.

Former J.C. Penney Store

Around 1943, the J.C. Penney store moved from the still-standing Dryden Building to its own location on the northeast corner of Saginaw and Kearsley Streets. It was Penney's only location in Flint, aside from the annex store in the former Hubbard Hardware building, until the store closed after the Christmas season of 1979, when Penney's opened new stores in January 1980 at the renamed Courtland Center and Genesee Valley. The signs were removed, and even the words *J.C. Penney* were removed from the terrazzo entrance floor. Plain concrete took their place. The building stood vacant until it was torn down in 1974.

Lost Bars and Restaurants

Also lost to Water Street Pavilion were popular downtown hangout spots, including Hat's Pub (formerly Brass Rail) on Kearsley Street and Doubie's on East First Street.

ALL OF THE ABOVE buildings, as well as all the structures in the area bounded by Riverbank Park to the north, Saginaw Street to the west, First Street to the south and Harrison Street to the east, were torn down to make way for the festival marketplace named Water Street Pavilion. The land south of Kearsley Street became a large parking lot dubbed the Flat

Lot, where various activities can be held. Water Street Pavilion opened in 1985. Alas, it was not successful, and it closed in 1990. University of Michigan–Flint bought it in 1993, and after renovations, it became the University Pavilion.

LOST TO THE ILL-FATED AUTOWORLD

The development of the ill-fated AutoWorld theme park in the early 1980s led to the clearing of a large area of Flint south of Fifth Avenue, east of Saginaw Street and west and north of the Flint River.

Fifth Avenue had an automotive supply store and a state unemployment office. Fourth Avenue had the Perry Printing Company. North Street (which was abandoned at the AutoWorld site) had the Riverfront Medical Center and the McDonald Dairy ice cream plant. The places that were lost along North Saginaw Street included the Lighthouse Restaurant, Greyhound Bus Terminal, General Tire Service store, Super City car wash, Sundance Lounge, Thor Sales & Service, Open Pantry Food Mart, Richardson Farm Dairy, Farr View Groceries, Flint Piston Service, Front Page bookstore, Genesee County substance abuse services office, Grandma's Treasures and La Gardenia Restaurant.

The most notable affected location was the Industrial Mutual Association (IMA) Auditorium, which was incorporated into AutoWorld. Built in 1929, the IMA Auditorium had a rich history as Flint's gathering place for major events. IMA was founded in 1922 by the merger of the Flint Vehicle Factories Mutual Benefit Association (which provided benefits in the event of sickness, injury or death of employees funded by worker contributions) and the Industrial Fellowship League (offering recreational and educational activities to workers).

IMA was located in the top five floors of the twelve-story Industrial Savings Bank Building (now part of Northbank Center). It provided a gymnasium, showers, bowling alleys, billiard parlors and well-appointed club rooms and lounges for auto workers and their families. A canopied balcony restaurant on the top floor allowed diners a view of Flint seen only by the copper lions that encircled the top of the building. Known as "IMA in the Clouds," the association's motto was "someplace to go in Flint."

By 1927, use by IMA members occasionally overcrowded the space used to hold basketball games, bowling, billiards and dancing, so plans were made to build a larger facility. The Randall Lumber Company was purchased that year. After the land was cleared, the IMA Auditorium was built, seating 6,266 people. Permanent theater seats were installed on the three arena sides of the auditorium, with the fourth side being the proscenium of the stage. The flexible main floor can be used for sporting events such as basketball, boxing and wrestling, dances, exhibitions and trade shows. It famously hosted the Shrine Circus each winter. Movable seats were used for stage events, concerts, conventions and movies, with a projection booth installed in the rear of the auditorium.

Backstage, the wings were three stories tall. The first floor consisted of a medical examiners room, steam room, rubbing room, the maintenance engineer's office and an ushers' lounge room. The second floor was for locker and shower rooms, and the third floor consisted of dressing rooms for the theatrical shows.

The IMA Auditorium freed up space in the Industrial Savings Bank building but would vacate the Industrial Savings Bank building a decade later.

In 1955, the IMA Auditorium's interior was renovated. In 1959, an annex with a hall seating nine hundred and a stage featuring a revolving floor

The IMA Auditorium, which became part of AutoWorld. *Author's collection.*

plus offices was completed. In 1966, a new covered walkway connecting the auditorium and annex was built with heat lamps to keep patrons warm during the cold winter months.

The IMA was funded through fees, payroll deductions and the IMA's vending operations inside factories, especially General Motors factories. Throughout the fifty years that the IMA Auditorium was in operation, it never made a profit. Changes in the automotive industry brought about by the 1970s energy crisis brought difficulties for the IMA. In 1977, the IMA Annex addition was gutted by a fire, causing at least $1 million in damage. Fire walls prevented the fire from spreading to the auditorium and offices. The cash-strapped IMA was unable to make repairs. But more significant was the loss of the IMA's vending contract with Buick, a contract it had had since 1917, which ended on April 1, 1979. So, the IMA could no longer afford to operate large arenas. The IMA Auditorium officially closed on June 18, 1979. The final major event held there was a June 1 concert by Peter Frampton.

The IMA Auditorium was sold to the Charles Stewart Mott Foundation and incorporated into AutoWorld, which opened on July 4, 1984. But paid attendance did not match projections, and AutoWorld was closed after two disappointing years. Open on occasion for special events and with the IMAX theater operating briefly, AutoWorld closed permanently by 1994. It was demolished when the former IMA Auditorium imploded in 1997.

Lost to Neglect

The Brownson-Fisher Building

Even though the story of this building was told in detail in *Hidden History of Flint*, it deserves to be mentioned here. After the W.A. Paterson Company closed in 1923, Paterson Factory no. 2, built in 1905 at the corner of Harrison and Third Streets, was sold in 1926. Apartments were planned, but an office building developed. It was the original home of the Flint Institute of Arts, and the ground floor became Brownson-Fisher Wallpaper & Paint. Even though the paint store was sold around 1963, the Brownson family kept ownership of the building. It received state historic recognition in 1981 and was listed in the National Register of Historic Placed in 1984.

It was sold in the 1990s. In 1996, the west wall of the building across Brush Alley from St. Paul's Episcopal Church collapsed, threatening that church and rendering the Brownson Building unsafe. Sold to the church, it was torn down and became the church's parking lot. They erected a low wall using the old bricks at the corner and installed a historic marker.

THEY DIDN'T BUILD HIGH-RISES IN THE 1960s LIKE THEY USED TO

Three notable high-rise buildings in downtown Flint were built in the late 1960s, but none of them survived more than half a century, proving that back then, they did not build them the way they used to.

The Voyager Inn

To prove one point, here is a hotel that was built in 1967 and was demolished in the early 1990s, while a competing hotel across the street, the Durant, was built in 1920, closed in 1973 and was neglected for decades. Because it was still structurally sound in 2008, it was renovated into apartments, which opened in 2010. The first hotel was the ten-story Voyager Inn, located at the corner of Detroit Street (now Martin Luther King Avenue) and First Avenue. In 1970, the mortgage on the hotel was foreclosed, and it became bank owned. One reason for the hotel's failure was a lack of parking. So, most of the buildings to the immediate north of it were purchased for parking in 1972. The reason for stating "most of the buildings" is because the owner of the former Jensen Music store held out for more money. The buildings around it were carefully demolished to save the remaining building. That building was eventually sold and demolished. Also in 1972, the Voyager Inn was renamed the Warwick Inn. In 1973, it was sold and received a Holiday Inn franchise, so it became a Holiday Inn after renovations. In 1975, it went into receivership and closed. New management reopened the Holiday Inn that year. It closed permanently the following year.

In 1977, the King's Daughters & Sons Home, which was forced to move from its Kearsley Street home for the aged to make way for the University

The Voyager Inn. *Courtesy of Michael Penzer.*

of Michigan–Flint, purchased the closed hotel. After renovations, Park Terrace officially opened in 1978. By 1980, Park Terrace doubled as a halfway house for youth offenders on probation. It closed by 1981. From around 1983 to 1987, it was student housing for nearby college students, called Riverfront Square. It closed by 1988. A target of vandals and scrappers, the stripped former hotel was torn down by the city in 1992. A vacant restaurant that had housed a McDonald's and then a Mega Coney Island is now standing where the Voyager Inn once stood.

Genesee Towers

In 1965, Genesee Merchants Bank & Trust Company announced construction of an eighteen-story office building, which would be Flint's tallest building. It was across Brush Alley from the previous tallest, Mott Foundation Building. Located at the corner of East First and Harrison Streets, demolition of several structures on the site commenced in 1966. Genesee Towers was completed in 1968. The University Club was located on the top floor, offering views of the city. In 1984, Genesee Bank was acquired by NBD Bancorp of Detroit, and in 1990, it officially assumed the NBD name. In 1997, NBD announced it was vacating Genesee Towers, which went through several owners over the years.

Over time, Genesee Towers' shoddy construction began to show. In 1981, a car hit a parking bumper in the parking garage portion of the tower, causing a concrete section to fall three stories from the side of the building to the ground. In a 1997 auction, the building's final owner bought it for $500,000. But that owner had neglected other buildings he owned and started neglecting this one as well. NBD vacated Genesee Towers in 1998. The following year, WDZZ radio vacated it. In 2001, the city cited Genesee Towers for numerous code violations. The number of tenants dwindled, and in 2002, barricades were put in place because debris was falling from the façade. After an expensive legal battle over the building's condemnation by then mayor Don Williamson and the value of Genesee Towers, the Michigan Supreme Court refused to hear the case, so the City of Flint had to buy Genesee Towers for $8 million in 2010. Every Flint property owner was charged an average of about $133 for a typical Flint home to pay for the city buying Genesee Towers.

The downtown Flint skyline in the 1980s, with Genesee Towers on the left. *Author's collection.*

On December 22, 2013, Genesee Towers was imploded. Video of the demolition was shot using multiple high-definition cameras, and local TV stations covered it live. It took about a year for the three-story pile of rubble to be cleared, and Harrison Street reopened after repairs in May 2015. An urban plaza with a large Flint sign is on the site today. (See the about the author photo)

YWCA on Third Street

In 1968, the YWCA moved to a new eight-story building offering additional facilities with emphasis placed on programs to serve women and children in the community, including swimming, fitness and exercise programs. The services the Flint YWCA offered changed with the times. Starting in 1975, women were allowed to use the facilities of the unaffiliated Flint YMCA. Originally founded as a place for women from farms and rural areas to stay in the city and find recreation, the YWCA

The YWCA on East Third Street during demolition. *Gary Flinn.*

now offers services including helping abused women, counseling and emergency shelter. But after nearly fifty years of use, the aging facility required additional maintenance, and by 2016, it was using only 10 percent of the 100,000-square-foot building. So, that year it moved to a renovated 10,500-square-foot space inside the Phoenix Building. The former YWCA was torn down in 2018 to make way for the Marketplace residential development with apartments and townhouses.

LOST INDUSTRY

General Motors Downsizing

Flint's economy over time rose and fell with the state of the automotive industry, which was the unfortunate result of Flint's economy being dependent on the automotive industry in general and General Motors in particular. But 1973 was the year when things began to gradually change, creating adverse effects to the people in Flint. It was the year of the Arab oil embargo, leading to rising gasoline prices and gas shortages, which changed the automotive marketplace in which car buyers were beginning to switch to more fuel-efficient vehicles leaving the domestic automotive industry and General Motors unprepared.

GM was also having reliability problems, as its vehicles were averaging nearly $500 million in annual warranty repairs. It also fell behind foreign auto makers regarding new emission rules. This allowed European auto makers as well as Japanese auto makers to increase their market share in America, slowing GM profits and laying the groundwork for GM's forthcoming downsizing of its manufacturing capacity in the Flint area.

The following are the affected General Motors factories in the Flint area in the order that demolition was completed.

AC Spark Plug, Industrial Avenue Plant: After losing control of the Boston-based Champion Spark Plug Company, which moved to Toledo, Ohio, Albert Champion moved to Flint, at the invitation of GM founder Billy Durant, to establish the Champion Ignition Company in 1908. It was initially based in a portion of the third floor of the Buick factory on Hamilton Avenue. The following year, it moved to its own two-story factory at the corner of Industrial Avenue and Harriet Street. In 1912, Champion greatly expanded the factory, and it was expanded further in 1915 and 1918. It eventually occupied both sides of Industrial Avenue, with two overhead walkways linking the factories and totaling 470,000 square feet on Industrial between Page and Harriet Streets. Because the Champion Spark Plug Company owned the Champion name, Albert Champion renamed the company AC Spark Plug in 1922. In 1925, Champion acquired the Dort Motor Company factory on North Dort Highway.

Champion died in 1927. In 1929, GM acquired Champion's interest in the company from his estate, and in 1933, the company officially became a division of GM. AC phased in production at the expanding east side factory complex and, over time, phased out portions of the Industrial Avenue factory complex, until it was closed in 1975 and torn down later that year, with demolition extending into 1976. Buick took over the site for parking.

Fisher One: In 1921, General Motors founder William C. "Billy" Durant founded Durant Motors and the following year broke ground on a new factory on Flint's southeast side at South Saginaw Street between Atherton and Hemphill Roads. This factory would build a car called the Flint, which would compete with GM's Buick line. Production at the $15 million factory began in 1923. But it proved to be too big for the volume of business, so it was sold to GM for $4 million in 1925 and became Fisher Body plant no. 1, building bodies for Buick that were then trucked to Buick on Flint's north side for final assembly. In 1984, GM changed its organizational structure, and the Fisher Body no. 1 plant became the Buick-Oldsmobile-Cadillac (B-O-C) Group Flint Body Assembly Plant.

The administration building is the last remaining part of Fisher Body plant no. 1 that is still intact. *Gary Flinn.*

Fisher Body plant no. 1. *Author's collection.*

To compete with global auto makers, GM completed renovations to the north side Buick complex, which led to the development of Buick City, inspired by the Toyota City complex in Japan. The switch to unibody construction and front wheel drive in new Buicks in 1985 made the B-O-C Flint Body Assembly plant expendable. The plant then shifted to building bodies for rear-wheel-drive Buick Regal, Chevrolet Monte Carlo and Oldsmobile Cutlass Supreme models for the Chevrolet-Pontiac-GM Canada (C-P-C) plant in Pontiac. But the closing of that assembly plant sealed the fate of old Fisher One.

The plant closed in December 1987. The closing was an inspiration for Michael Moore's first film, *Roger & Me*. After partial demolition and renovations, the site became the Great Lakes Technology Centre. Only the old factory's administration building maintained its original exterior.

Fisher Coldwater Road: The Fisher Body Coldwater Road plant in Genesee Township opened in 1953 and was built for the Buick Motor Division. The original plan was to build aircraft engines for the Korean War. But the end of that war led the plant, still under construction at that time, to be turned over to GM's Ternstedt Division and used for civilian production of body hardware. The Detroit-based Ternstedt Manufacturing Company developed the first dependable closed car window regulator. By 1920, Ternstedt was a subsidiary of Fisher Body, which became a wholly owned subsidiary of GM in 1926, making Ternstedt a GM division. Ternstedt was absorbed into Fisher Body in 1969. The 1.8-million-square-foot plant employed 1,900 people and produced power and manual window regulators, door and deck lid hinges and headliners.

GM's 1984 organizational structure dissolved Fisher Body, and the Coldwater Road plant became part of GM's new Fisher Guide parts division. In 1989, Fisher Guide merged with GM's Inland Division to become GM's Inland Fisher Guide Division. Inland Fisher Guide became part of GM's spinoff Delphi Automotive Systems in 1995. The following year, Delphi sold the plant to Peregrine Inc. But the Coldwater Road plant was unprofitable, and it closed in 1998. It was torn down shortly afterward, leading to estimated losses of $1 million in tax revenue. As of this writing, a landfill behind the former site is being monitored for ground water contamination.

Buick City: In 1898, Billy Durant of the Durant-Dort Carriage Company purchased the 220-acre William Hamilton farm from his daughter, Minnie Loranger, for $22,000. In 1907, Durant's new three-story factory for his Buick Motor Company was built, consolidating manufacturing from factories in Jackson, Michigan, and west of downtown Flint. That was the start of what would become a sprawling complex of factories on Flint's north side. Buick was the foundation company leading to the formation of General Motors by Durant in 1908, which was also the year that the Buick plant became the largest automobile factory in

What later became Buick City in its early years. *Author's collection.*

the world. Over the years, additional factories would be built on the site. In a reorganization of the Buick factory complex in the mid-1980s, the sprawling site stretching from Pierson Road to the north, the CSX railroad tracks to the east, Harriet Street to the south and Industrial Avenue to the west would become Buick City.

By the 1980s, Buick sales were declining rapidly. In 1997, it was announced that Buick City would close. On June 29, 1999, a Buick LeSabre was the final car to roll off the Buick City assembly line. Demolition of the complex would begin afterward. A few factory buildings manufacturing engines and transmissions plus support buildings north of Leith Street were saved to become the GM Powertrain Flint North complex.

Chevy in the Hole/Fisher Guide/AC Flint West: For a century and a half, beginning in 1865, a site west of downtown along the Flint River was an industrial area, beginning with lumber processing before moving to wagon and carriage building and culminating in automotive manufacturing. What became known as Chevy in the Hole by 1934 covered eighty acres and employed fourteen thousand workers at thirty-one factories on both sides of the river. An overhead tunnel above Chevrolet Avenue became a local landmark, topped on both sides by Chevrolet's bow tie sign in neon.

Activity began winding down in 1984 when Plant 4, the engine plant, closed. That same year, a General Motors reorganization led to the complex becoming part of the C-P-C Group. When the complex was taken over by GM's Fisher Guide division by 1986, the bow tie signs came down and were moved to the Vic Canever Chevrolet dealership in Fenton. In 1987, AC took over the complex, and Delphi took over in 1995. Vacant buildings were torn down one by one, beginning in 1995 with the old Fisher Body no. 2 plant. The powerhouse was demolished in 1999, and the twin smokestacks were demolished on March 6. Delphi Plant 10 and the Water Treatment Plant were demolished in 2003. The repurposed Delphi Plant 4 was the last building closed on July 2, 2004, and demolition began shortly afterward. Delphi did not remove equipment and confidential medical records before demolition began, so it exposed everything for all to find, reported by the *Uncommon Sense* alternative newspaper in 2005.

Kettering University took over the site north of the river for campus expansion, and Kettering's GM Mobility Research Center now occupies part of the site. Kettering also took over Plant 35, which, after renovations, became the C.S. Mott Engineering and Science Center. The City of Flint took over the site south of the river, which became parkland called Chevy

A vintage photo of the Chevy in the Hole overhead tunnel above Chevrolet Avenue. *Courtesy of Marlene Keller.*

Chevy in the Hole. *Author's collection.*

Commons after brownfield cleanup. One GM manufacturing facility remains in operation—the old Plant 38 on Stevenson Street is now Flint Tool and Die.

GM Powertrain V8 Engine Plant: Part of Chevrolet Motor Division's post–World War II expansion, the V8 Engine Plant was built in 1953 on Van Slyke Road southwest of Flint. At that time, each GM division had its own engine manufacturing operations. That changed in 1984 with GM's first reorganization with the Van Slyke engine plant part of the C-P-C (Chevrolet-Pontiac-GM Canada) Group, which was combined with the B-O-C (Buick-Oldsmobile-Cadillac) Group's engine operations in 1990 to form the GM Engine Division. That was combined with the GM Hydra-Matic division, which made transmissions, in 1990, creating GM Powertrain. In 1999, GM Powertrain closed the V8 Engine Plant, and it was replaced by the new Flint Engine South Plant, just south of the V8 Engine Plant, which was demolished shortly afterward. A paint shop addition to the GM Flint Assembly Plant now occupies the site.

GM Powertrain Flint North: When most of the Buick City complex was closed down, the remaining buildings north of Leith Street, which made automotive components, were saved. The oldest-surviving factory building was built in 1926–27 as Factory 70 and served as a foundry until 1980. It was remodeled in 1980–81 and renamed Factory 81, making transmission components, pistons and torque converter vanes. The other factories in the complex were Factory 36, engine component manufacturing and assembly; Factory 10, transmission and engine component manufacturing; and Factory 5, transmission component and hinge manufacturing. Support buildings were Building 18, personnel, hospital and the fire department; Building 21, machine shop and tool regrind; Building 22, the powerhouse behind Factory 10; Building 55, waste treatment; Building 86, the Worldwide Facilities Group; and what was left of Factory 3, which was renovated into the cultural and diversity center, opened in 2004.

In 2008, the final 3.8-liter V6 engine was built on the site. At that time, Flint North employed more than 1,200 workers. Two years later, the rest of the complex, employing around 400 workers, was closed. This brought to an end a century of manufacturing at what became Buick City, where in the mid-1950s, 29,400 people were employed. The remaining buildings were torn down shortly afterward.

AC Flint East: As previously mentioned, Albert Champion acquired the Dort Motor Company plant on North Dort Highway in 1925 for his AC Spark Plug factory. After Champion died in 1927, GM acquired his interest in the company, taking it over in 1929 and becoming a GM division in 1933. Over time, the factory complex on North Dort Highway sprawled eastward all the way to Center Road uninterrupted and even extended into Burton. After AC took over the former Chevy in the Hole factories in 1987 (becoming AC Flint West), this complex became known as AC Flint East.

In 1988, GM merged the AC Spark Plug division with the Rochester Products Division to form AC Rochester, which was initially based at Flint East before the headquarters was moved to the Great Lakes Technology Centre. Another GM divisional consolidation led to the formation of AC Delco Systems in 1994. The following year, it was absorbed into GM's spinoff company, Delphi Automotive Systems, which was separated from GM in 1999. Delphi's bankruptcy in 2005 led to plans to close most of its American plants, including Flint East. The decline in employment at the Flint East complex has been gradual from around 7,000 in 1996 to 3,500 in 2003 to about 1,100 in 2008. In 2007, the engineering center at the corner of Davison Road and Averill Avenue was closed, with the jobs shifted to Auburn Hills.

Demolition began in April 2008 and included most of the Flint East complex from Dort Highway eastward to Averill Avenue, including the power plant and engineering and research center. Before the historic factory, built in 1928 at the corner of Dort Highway and Davison Road, was razed, an expert at removing tiles carefully removed Flint Faience tiles, including a Flint Faience Tiles tile sign, from the façade in June 2008. Flint Faience & Tile Company was a GM subsidiary that operated from 1921 to 1933, using kilns that were normally used for spark plug insulators when spark plugs were not being made. The tiles were installed in homes, schools and businesses, until production of tiles was discontinued as demand for spark plugs increased. The surviving tiles are now collectible. The Adamo Group of Detroit was the demolition contractor and completed demolition in August 2009. This left the large factory building that was built in stages extending from Averill Avenue to Center Road along Robert T. Longway Boulevard. That closed in 2013, when the work the remaining 287 employees did was shifted to Mexico. The portion of the factory facing Center Road was demolished the following year. In 2017, the remaining part of the old factory on Averill and Longway was sold and part of it is now used by Genesee Packaging.

One of the last remaining buildings of the old AC Spark Plug complex at the corner of Averill Avenue and Robert T. Longway Boulevard. *Gary Flinn.*

MORE LOST INDUSTRIES

Paramount Potato Chips

Around 1949, Edward S. Dewan founded the Paramount Potato Chip Company at G-3300 South Dort Highway in what was then Burton Township, now the city of Burton. It manufactured potato chips and offered tours of the plant.

In 1958, Robert N. Johnson, who was working as a plant manager at Buckeye Potato Chips in Columbus, Ohio, moved to Flint and bought the Paramount Potato Chip Company. In 1962, the company moved to a newly constructed plant in the city of Flint just east of South Dort Highway, at 2727 Lippincott Boulevard.

Heavily advertising on TV, radio and newspapers, Paramount Potato Chips prospered in the 1960s, doubling its output in a mid-decade expansion, enhanced by a potato chip mascot cowboy named Slim Chiply, who was inspired by the Buckeye Potato Chips mascot. His cowboy garb was inspired by Johnson's young son Clark, who was going through a cowboy stage. The bright red package bore the words "Slim Chiply says 'Reach' for Full Flavor."

Old timers might recall this jingle:

[Slim Chiply] Reach, stranger!
[Solo singer] For Paramount Potato Chips
[Slim Chiply] I'm Slim Chiply, the guy you see
[chorus] On the Paramount Potato Chips bright red pack
[Slim Chiply] I'm the flavor deputy, protecting crispness in every sack
[chorus] They're delicious and so nutritious
[Slim Chiply] Yes, sirree, they're pips
[chorus] Paramount Potato Chips

Because potato chips are by nature a delicate product to produce and distribute, potato chip manufacturers initially marketed only to local and regional areas. Paramount was marketed in Flint and surrounding areas in a fifty-mile radius, including Saginaw and Lansing. One notable competitor was Detroit-based Nicolay-Dancey Inc., which marketed New Era potato chips. It expanded outside Michigan, but to do that, it opened branch factories to manufacture potato chips outside Michigan and became a regional powerhouse.

In 1958, the maker of Fritos corn chips bought Nicolay-Dancey for $4 million. In 1961, Fritos merged with potato chip maker H.W. Lay & Company to create Frito-Lay. The New Era brand was phased out by the mid-1960s in favor of Lay's potato chips. This helped make Lay's a national potato chip brand, causing headaches for the local and regional companies, such as Paramount.

In the 1980s, two major manufactures, food supplier Borden and beer brewer Anheuser-Busch, tried to muscle into the potato chip market with Borden and Eagle snacks, respectively. That put a premium on shelf space, which did not help the smaller chip makers. Both Borden and Anheuser-Busch were ultimately unsuccessful, and both exited the snack food business in the 1990s.

A series of setbacks starting in the 1980s led to Paramount's demise. First was the loss of business from Meijer and Kroger, along with other private label contracts. Then in 1991, major buyer Hamady Brothers Food Markets went out of business, and Paramount lost a sex discrimination lawsuit in which the company was ordered to pay more than $192,000 to several female employees. On April 9, 1992, twenty-two teamster members went on strike after they lost their medical benefits when the company failed to pay health insurance premiums. On Tuesday, April 14, the Paramount Potato Chip Company closed after NBD Bank seized its assets, leaving forty employees out of work.

Bay City–based Made Rite Potato Chips hired several of the Paramount drivers and Paramount's shelf space was taken up by Made Rite chips. The following June, the Detroit-based makers of Better Made Potato Chips bought the rights to market Paramount potato chips, including the Slim Chiply mascot. Distribution was limited because Made Rite had already taken over shelf space. In 1994, Better Made bought Made Rite, converting the Made Rite plant into a distribution warehouse and expanding Better Made marketing to cover most of Michigan.

In 2008, the Genesee County Community Action Agency bought the former Paramount Potato Chips plant at 2727 Lippincott for $1 million, and it now houses the Genesee County Community Action Resource Department

Du Pont Flint Plant

In 1901, the Durant-Dort Carriage Company founded Flint Varnish Works to supply paints and finishes for the company, with J. Dallas Dort as its president. In 1909, the company became independent of Durant-Dort and was renamed the Flint Varnish & Color Works, with William W. Mountain as general manager. In 1910, Flint Varnish began supplying paint for the automotive industry after expanding into a three-story factory, which also served the railroad industry. In 1913, the company increased its capitalization to $1 million, and Mountain was chosen as the new president while continuing as general manager. Business had doubled in the past few months. Dort continued serving as a director, and General Motors president Charles W. Nash became a director.

In 1918, DuPont acquired control of Flint Varnish & Color Works, and Mountain continued as president and general manager. Over the years, the DuPont paint factory would expand outward to St. John and Wood Streets and absorb the Marvel Carburetor Company, as well as an old brewery. The factory also had a specialty plant that produced Rally and No. 7 products, as well as Duco cement. In 1985, rival finishes supplier PPG Industries established a coatings campus in Flint after becoming a paint supplier for GM. A decade later, DuPont purchased a large paint plant in Mount Clemens from Ford Motor Company, and the resulting consolidation led DuPont to close its historic paint plant at 1555 James

P. Cole Boulevard across Hamilton Avenue from Buick City, and it was demolished shortly afterward.

Helmac Products Corp.

In 1955, Nicholas McKay and his wife, Helen, had to chaperone a school dance. Nicholas had forgotten to take his sport coat to the cleaners, so it was covered in lint. Using a discarded toilet paper roll, masking tape and a mangled wire coat hanger, he managed to clean off the lint. In 1956, Nicholas McKay invented the lint roller. At that time, he was business manager for Reliance Electrical and Engineering. He filed for a patent in 1957 and received it in 1963. He and Helen founded Helmac, named after Helen, by 1959. By 1962, they had set up shop in downtown Flint at 336 West First Street. By 1968, they had moved to a newly constructed factory at 528 Kelso Street. That year, the Helmac Lint Pic-Up lint roller achieved national distribution. By 1973, it was available at more than sixty thousand retail locations.

In 1993, Harvard Business School graduate Nicholas McKay Jr. joined the company. Under his guidance, additional products were introduced. The lint roller appeared in the 1988 film *The Accidental Tourist* and more notably in Michael Moore's 1989 film *Roger & Me*. At that time, the Kelso Avenue plant employed around seventy-five people.

In 1998, the 3M Company introduced its own competing lint roller. A brand consultant suggested adopting a catchier brand name, and the Evercare brand was adopted, replacing the Helmac brand. Unable to receive tax incentives in 1999 to expand further, the company moved to the Atlanta, Georgia suburb of Alpharetta. In 2004, Butler Home Products of Marlborough, Massachusetts, bought the company, and later that year, Nicholas McKay Sr. died on November 15 in Phoenix, Arizona, at age ninety-three. The former plant on Kelso Street is now home to automotive supplier Attentive Industries.

Flint Sausage Works (Salay's Meats)

In 1916, Emil Salay Sr. moved to Flint from Pomona, California, settling at 1210 Avenue A, where he founded the Flint Sausage Works with his wife, Mary. By 1923, he had built up enough business to move the

Vintage Helmac Lint Pic-Up window ad.

Flint Sausage Works to its long-time address at 1517 St. John Street, just south of the DuPont paint plant. For several decades, the company, which produced Salay's meat products, was a rival to Koegel Meats. The Salays had seven children. Emil Salay Jr. was just a toddler when the Flint Sausage Works, also known as Salay's Inc., was established. His entire working career was with Salay's Meats, eventually becoming president and CEO. When James P. Cole Boulevard was developed on the west side of the Flint River, replacing sections of St. John Street, Flint Sausage Works wound up located at a dead-end north of Wood Street. The younger Salay retired from the company in 2000, living to the ripe old age of one hundred. Unfortunately, the company he led folded in 2003, making Koegel's the top dog in Flint.

McDonald Dairy

When brothers John and William McDonald bought the Independent Dairy Company in 1929, there were fourteen dairy firms operating. In 1931, they built the McDonald Dairy plant on Lewis Street, now Chavez Drive, which expanded numerous times over the years. In 1942, they reorganized the company into a nonprofit cooperative eventually owned by the milk producers, and the McDonalds continued to run the company. John McDonald died in 1947, leaving William in sole command. In 1950, a separate ice cream plant was built at 602 Payne (later North) Street. It was eventually torn down for the ill-fated AutoWorld. The company acquired additional dairies to expand its marketing area. William McDonald retired in 1962 and died in 1979.

McDonald Dairy developed financial problems, leading to a $1.82 million loss in 1976, despite record sales. It was sold in 1979 to the Michigan Milk Producers Association. In November 1986, it sold the dairy to Grand Rapids–based Country Fresh Dairy. By 2000, Country Fresh dropped the McDonald brand. In 2002, the McDonald sign was replaced by a Country Fresh sign. The company closed the Flint plant in 2009, and production shifted to plants in Grand Rapids and Livonia. The former McDonald Dairy plant was sold in 2017 to C3 Venture Flint, which demolished the older portions of the complex. There are plans for modular housing to be built there.

Soft Drink Bottling Plants

In the 1970s, Flint had four soft drink bottling plants. Now there are none, as the beverages are now shipped to the area and delivered to stores from local distribution warehouses. Flint's best known local bottling company produced M&S beverages. It was founded in 1918 by Morris Weinstein and Samuel Buckler, who worked for what is now Faygo in Detroit. It was best known for being the local bottler for 7Up. The Weinstein family bought Buckler's interest in 1944, and the company was sold in 1969. It came under local ownership again in 1985, when the BFW Bottling Company was established by area car dealers Al Bennett and Mel Farr and Detroit attorney Charles Wells. They were unable to compete effectively with Coke and Pepsi, and the company was absorbed in 1988 by a larger 7Up bottler based in Holland, Michigan, which kept the plant operating until it closed in 1989. Buckler founded the Buckler Beverage Company, which produced Squirt, Dr Pepper, Crush and other brands until it folded in 1981.

Pepsi-Cola products were marketed in Flint as early as 1938, but it was not bottled locally until 1966, when the Pepsi bottling plant opened at 500 South Averill Avenue. By the time it closed around 1995, it was the last bottling plant in Michigan that produced Pepsi products in refillable glass bottles.

Today, the old Coca-Cola bottling plant at 2515 Lapeer Road functions as a distribution warehouse operated by Great Lakes Coca-Cola. But when it opened at 2515 Lapeer Road around 1937, it replaced a plant on North Saginaw Street. It expanded numerous times over the years, including a 1997 addition that was built after the old Buckler Beverage plant next door was torn down. When the Coca-Cola bottling lines were shut down at the start of 2009, that ended production of soft drinks in the Flint area. The reason the plant lasted as long as it did was easy access to the I-69 expressway off Dort Highway, also the reason why the former plant is now Coca-Cola's distribution warehouse.

The other soft drink distribution warehouses are also near expressways, Pepsi-Cola at 6200 Taylor Drive in Mundy Township and 7Up Flint operating as the American Bottling Company at 7300 Enterprise Parkway off Mount Morris Road in Mount Morris Township.

LOST MEDIA

Four Flint radio stations can be considered lost. The following are the stations in the order that they first went on air.

WFDF

Flint's pioneering radio station was WFDF, which first went on air in 1922 as WEAA and changed its call letters to the initials of the station's founder, Frank D. Fallain, in 1925. I told the full story of this pioneering radio station in my first book, *Remembering Flint, Michigan.* In 2002, the station's owner, Cumulus Media, received an offer from the ABC division of the Walt Disney Company that it could not refuse, and WFDF was sold for $3 million. It became the southeast Michigan outlet for Radio Disney and increased the station's range by buying another radio station near Toledo, Ohio, and taking it off air to expand its signal and move the station to the Detroit area. The city of license moved to the Detroit suburb of Farmington Hills. In 2014, Radio Disney changed its focus to streaming audio via the internet and sold most of its stations, including WFDF. Currently owned by Adell Broadcasting and based in the Detroit suburb of Southfield, the station can

WTAC Music Guide giving its top 30 hits and the six hit-bound records for the week of July 10, 1970. *Author's collection.*

still be received in Flint and has an urban talk format. It is called 910 AM Superstation.

WTAC

The second radio station to go on air in Flint was the station that brought rock-and-roll music to the town. WTAC The Big 600 first went on the air in 1946. It was cofounded by George W. Trendle (creator of the *Lone Ranger*) and H. Allen Campbell. The original call letters were WTCB, for Trendle-Campbell Broadcasting. The company briefly operated a TV station, WTAC-TV channel 16, in 1953–54, which failed. In 1956, the station brought rock and roll to Flint with a top 40 format. It served the area for decades, until the rise of FM radio led to the station's decline by the end of the 1970s. It changed its format to country music in 1981, but that was not successful. The station's last hurrah came when it was sold and evolved into a talk and oldies stations, saying WeeTac Is Back.

One of the talk shows developed a following. It was hosted by Estelle Kaufman, wife of Dr. Benjamin Kaufman (who owned the station with his family) and mother-in-law of former radio newscaster (WWCK 105 FM, WTRX and WFDF), attorney and future Genesee County prosecutor David Leyton. Called *Estelle & Friends*, it was funny, interesting, and a bit off beat. She played songs from the '40s and '50s between guests. But competition for a standalone AM station is tough, with FM stations receiving higher ratings. In 1989, the station was sold and adopted a Christian format, eventually changing its call letters to WSNL. Kaufman's show began airing after the station was sold but before the sale was approved. Leyton recalled that if he had known that his mother-in-law's show would catch on, the family wouldn't have sold the station.

The station's four-tower array was located in Grand Blanc Township on Center Road south of Hill Road. The land became very valuable, so in 2003, it was sold, and three of the four towers were taken down. The station operated at reduced power with the remaining tower while a new four-tower array was built in Gaines Township next to the old Berlin & Farro toxic waste site. When the new transmitting facilities became operational, the remaining tower went down, and the Grand Blanc site is now the Cambridge Park condominium development.

WFBE

The Flint Board of Education put FM radio station WFBE on the air on October 5, 1953. It provided in-school educational programs to students. One of the programs WFBE produced won the coveted George Foster Peabody award in 1970. The following year, WFBE began to receive funding from the Corporation for Public Broadcasting, allowing the station to broadcast from 6:00 a.m. to midnight. During most of its time as a public radio station, it operated from studios and offices in the lower level of Flint Central High School. Unlike most educational stations, WFBE operated on a commercial frequency at 95.1 MHz. Over time, the station was able to upgrade its facilities with the help of fundraising. In the late 1970s, it began broadcasting in stereo

Stephen All and Susan Kilmer report the news of the week for Flint elementary school students in the mid-1960s at WFBE-FM's Studio A. Located in the lower level of Central High School, the *FBE* in WFBE stood for "Flint Board of Education." *Courtesy of Wendy All.*

and then increased its power. It eventually increased its effective radiated power to the maximum allowed. But Flint Schools' financial problems led the Flint Board of Education to sell WFBE to a commercial operator for $7 million in 1997. The Sloan Museum received more than two thousand tape recordings, as well as vintage equipment after the sale.

It became a country music station called Nash FM, which it still is today. The studios were first moved to an office building on Miller Road. It was sold again, and in 2012, it was moved to Taylor Drive in Mundy Township, sharing space with other co-owned radio stations. In 2010, the station's transmitters were moved from Central High School to the co-owned WTRX (AM) transmitter building on Bristol Road near Dort Highway in Burton. During renovation of the WTRX facilities, the old WTRX office wing was razed, and the old WTRX studio space was gutted to make way for additional transmitting equipment. A new transmitting antenna was mounted on the tall WTRX tower. After the move, the old tower at Central High was taken down, cut up and put in a dumpster placed in Central's parking lot.

WWCK-FM

WWCK-FM began broadcasting in 1964 as WMRP-FM, the sister station of WMRP AM 1570 (now WWCK-AM). It was originally owned by Methodist Radio Parish, with a religious and middle-of-the-road music format. The two stations simulcasted until new regulations led to separate programming. The FM station then played top 40 music. But when the FM station began broadcasting in stereo, the engineer had trouble modifying the master control console, so the stereo signal was turned off when music was not played, and the stereo signal was turned back on when the music resumed.

The stations were sold in 1971, when the United Methodist Church withdrew its support. The new owners changed the call letters of both stations. While the AM station had different calls over the years, the FM station's WWCK remained constant. It originally had top 40 music during the day and a rock music format at night. In 1975, the station was sold, and the FM station switched to an album-oriented rock music format full time. After a couple of years of tweaking the format, it developed into a ratings powerhouse, enjoying high ratings for several years and becoming widely noticed nationally. One program, *Buffalo Dick's Radio Ranch*, went into national syndication. On Sunday mornings, Michael Moore of future *Roger & Me* fame hosted *Radio Free Flint*.

WWCK's former studio location on Lapeer Road, where the station's transmitters are still located. *Gary Flinn.*

Competition on both sides of the musical spectrum cut into ratings in the late 1980s, with WIOG's top 40 music and WCRZ Cars 108's adult contemporary. So, in 1988, the station was sold, and the new owners switched to top 40 music as CK105.5. Despite protests from listeners, the station garnered higher ratings. But the national profile was gone. A documentary released on the internet, *Flint's Best Rock*, gave the story of 105 FM.

WFUM-TV/WCMZ-TV

Flint was probably the last major American city not served by its own noncommercial public TV station. That ended when the University of Michigan–Flint launched WFUM-TV channel 28 on August 23, 1980. Until then, Flint viewers with outdoor TV antennas were able to watch PBS programs from the Saginaw area on WUCM-TV channel 19 from the campus of Delta College in University Center, WKAR-TV channel 23 from the campus of Michigan State University in East Lansing and

The final sign-off for the now defunct PBS station serving Flint, WCMZ-TV, on April 23, 2018.

WTVS channel 56 from Detroit. Flint cable TV subscribers could pick up some of these channels. But in 2009, the University of Michigan decided to discontinue operations of WFUM-TV and sold the station to Central Michigan University, which operates WCMU-TV from Mount Pleasant. WCMU took over operations of WFUM-TV the following year, simulcasting WCMU-TV's signal and changing the Flint station's call letters to WCMZ-TV.

When the Federal Communications Commission (FCC) mandated the conversion of TV stations to digital broadcasting with the phasing out of analog TV broadcasts in 2009, Delta College (now with call letters WDCQ) decided to consolidate its two TV transmitters (including Bad Axe–licensed station WUCX, later WDCP, with its transmitter outside Ubly). They would become one digital transmitter located on Quanicassee Road north of Reese, with a strong signal reaching Flint. Called Delta College Public Media, it served Bad Axe, Bay City, Midland, Saginaw and Flint. On February 8, 2017, CMU announced it would sell WCMZ-TV in the FCC spectrum auction for $14,163,505, citing the easy availability of surrounding PBS member stations, including WKAR-TV. WCMZ-TV went off the air permanently at 11:59 p.m. on April 23, 2018.

The Flint Journal

The *Flint Journal* was Flint's only daily newspaper until 2009, when it cut its staff and reduced publication to three times a week, later adding a fourth day in 2010. The paper is now produced on Sunday, Tuesday, Thursday and Friday. It also consolidated the printing plants of its co-owned newspapers, maintaining the Grand Rapids plant and selling the Flint production and distribution center. That has since been renovated and became the new location of the Flint Farmers Market.

Readers were directed to turn to MLive.com to get caught up on news stories. It sometimes took days for a story reported online to appear in print. This writer contributed monthly history pieces to the *Flint Journal* and its co-owned *Your Magazine* until the cutbacks, which included shutting down *Your Magazine*. The newspaper also moved from its historic office at the corner of First and Harrison Streets to a storefront on South Saginaw Street. The former office became the Michigan State University College of Human Medicine.

LOST TRADITIONS

Central v. Northern on Thanksgiving Day

After Flint's second high school, Northern, opened in 1928, a crosstown rivalry with the former Flint High School, renamed Central, began, starting a Thanksgiving tradition that lasted almost fifty years.

The first Thanksgiving Day football game was played at Dort Memorial Field, on the Central High School grounds, on November 29, 1928. It attracted eight thousand fans who saw a strong defensive game that ended in the Northern Eskimos (later Vikings) defeating the Central Red-Blacks (later Indians) 7-0 on a Central fumble to win the Wildanger Trophy.

The second game was held at Northern, where seven thousand braved the cold to see Northern win again with a score of 6-0. Two field goals by right guard Frank Mitoraj were the difference in another strong defensive game.

The 1930 game was the first one at the new Atwood Stadium, and Northern continued its domination of the series by defeating Central 18-0, thanks to all-state Northern quarterback Russ Reynolds. This time, 9,500 fans attended. It wasn't until 1931 that Central head coach Dan Fisher finally coached the team to a victory, defeating Guy Houston's Northern team 6-0 to claim the Wildanger Trophy for the first time. Houston had a long coaching tenure at Northern, beginning when the school opened until 1951, when he won his final game.

The Thanksgiving game attracted at least 10,000 fans for thirty-two straight games, from 1932 to 1967. The 1947 game was noted for playing conditions more suited for dog sledding, with snow covering the frozen field. Central coach Howard Auer had his team switch to basketball shoes after the first quarter, which helped Central beat Northern 20-6 and finish the season undefeated. In the only tie game, 13-13, in 1948, there were 20,300 fans at Atwood Stadium. The 1949 game was another snowy one, with Northern beating Central 13-0. Northern halfback Leroy Bolden scored both touchdowns. The largest crowd at Atwood Stadium was 20,600 in 1950 to see Northern beat Central by a score of 20-13. Bolden ran seventy-nine yards for the winning touchdown with less than three minutes to play. There was no time for tailgating, as the game was an early afternoon affair to allow families to enjoy traditional Thanksgiving dinners.

In 1975, the Michigan High School Athletic Association decided to begin a playoff system for high school football teams, ending the Thanksgiving Day tradition. The forty-ninth and final Thanksgiving game matchup between Northern and Central in 1976 was also the only overtime game. Central beat Northern 7-6 in front of only 3,947 at Atwood Stadium. The game was scoreless in regulation. In overtime, Central scored a touchdown first and kicked the extra point. Northern then scored a touchdown and attempted a two-point conversion pass, which was batted away for Central's final game win. Northern won more Thanksgiving games, twenty-eight to Central's twenty.

Fans were not content with the Thanksgiving Day tradition ending after forty-nine games. On Thanksgiving Day 1977, the Nostalgia Bowl was held at Atwood to close the series and make it an even fifty games. Michael Cherveny, 1935 Northern graduate, was one of two known fans who attended every Northern-Central Thanksgiving game. The other was Central graduate Ted Vaughan, and both attended the Nostalgia Bowl. It was organized by alumni of both high schools as a touch football game. It was a final tribute to players, marching band members, cheerleaders, coaches, officials and fans who made the event a classic through the years. Central won the game 12-0, despite Northern's "protest" of a "sleeper" play, which provided the winning score of this fun contest.

The January Burning of the Greens

In 1953, a tradition to officially end the holiday season began. On the traditional Twelfth Night, January 6, Christmas trees that were gathered in Kearsley Park were burned in a set of bonfires called the "Burning of the Greens." January 6 also marks the Christian festival of the Epiphany. It is thought that the tradition of burning Christmas trees on the Twelfth Night began in Germany, where the Christmas tree tradition began.

There were two purposes to the Burning of the Greens ceremony. Along with the colorful tradition, it also provided a safe and efficient means for the community to dispose of its Christmas greenery. There were sixteen Burning of the Greens events, beginning in 1953. In 1954, there was a debate about which chemical to use to enhance the display of the flames. Calcium chloride was used, which produced an orange flame. Other chemicals used to enhance fires are copper sulphate, which produces a green flame, and nitrate, which produces a red flame.

The 1954 Burning of the Greens attracted a crowd of three thousand, watching more than two thousand trees burn. In 1955, it was held early on January 4 because of a conflict with a Northern-Central basketball game scheduled for January 6. In 1967, high winds delayed the Burning of the Greens until January 9. Christmas carols were sung by local children before the fires were set, and in 1969, there was a firework display, plus a pageant about Christmas traditions. On the final Burning of the Greens on January 6, 1970, more than seven thousand trees were burned. The tradition ended after a city air pollution control ordinance was enacted in April 1970. It was estimated that in seventeen years, the Burning of the Greens burned 125,000 trees. Trees the city collected after Christmas 1970 went through the chipper.

LOST SCHOOLS

The Flint School District rose with the growth of the automobile industry and fell with the industry's decline in the area. In the 1913–14 school year, enrollment was 8,091 students. It would rise steadily over the years, with several schools built in the 1920s, prior to the Great Depression. Additional schools were built in the 1950s during the post–World War II baby boom through the 1970s.

In the mid-1930s, during the Great Depression, Flint Schools pioneered the community school concept. Schools operated during evenings and weekends even during the summer to provide social activities for both children and adults. Conceived by physical education instructor Frank Manley, the program was funded by General Motors board member Charles Stewart Mott through his Mott Foundation.

Restrictive covenants in place until the 1960s in most subdivisions limited where Black people could live to the Floral Park and St. John Street neighborhoods. The Flint Board of Education also practiced racial segregation in the way elementary school boundaries were drawn, especially in the 1950s. The board even isolated a Black second grader in a closet at Homedale School after complaints from White parents in 1959. As enrollment swelled in the 1950s and 1960s, Flint Schools built primary units resembling ranch houses in neighborhoods, often near school boundaries. From 1950 until 1966, 116 primary units were built, usually four in a neighborhood, serving kindergarten through third grade. When the primary units were no longer needed, they were sold and were usually converted into private homes, although primary units in zoned commercial areas often became commercial businesses.

Enrollment peaked with 47,867 students for the 1967–68 school year and then began to decline as some Flint families moved to suburban areas. Enrollment fell to 38,086 for the 1977–78 school year, with a combination of the middle-class flight to the suburbs and the beginning of factory closings. Enrollment to 29,556 students for the 1990–91 school year. With the popularity of privately owned charter schools, enrollment fell even more rapidly. The 2004–5 school year saw enrollment fall to 19,204. Enrollment fell below 10,000 for the 2012–13, with 9,585 students. The 2015–2016 school year saw 4,875 students enrolled.

As the 1970s began, enrollment at some schools was still swelling. In 1969, Williams School was built to replace two schools: the predominately Black Roosevelt School, which was in the path of the I-475 expressway, and the predominately White Lewis School, which was annexed by the adjacent Lowell Junior High School to relieve overcrowding. In 1971, a new Northern High School opened to relieve overcrowding at a campus that had contained the old Northern High School, Emerson Junior High School and Garfield Elementary School. Under the new arrangement, Garfield served kindergarten through fourth grades; Emerson Junior High became Emerson Intermediate School, serving fifth through seventh; grades and the old Northern became the new Emerson Junior High, serving eighth and ninth graders. Three new elementary schools were built in the early 1970s, King and Summerfield Schools in 1970 and Wilkins in 1972. Roosevelt was used for special education programs until it was torn down in 1974 to make way for I-475.

In 1971, declining enrollment led to the closure of Clark School, due to nearby expressway interchange construction, and Fairview School because the St. John Street neighborhood was being wiped by out I-475 construction and urban renewal. Fairview was then leased to the Genesee County Regional Drug Abuse Commission. Increasing maintenance costs led to the closure of Flint's oldest elementary school, built in 1902, Doyle School.

The Opportunities Industrial Center (OIC) leased the school, but it was abandoned by 1977. Two other aging schools closed in 1976, Oak School, built in 1908, and Parkland School, built in 1913. The Flint Police briefly used Oak for community programs, and Parkland housed the Whitney M. Young Jr. Street Academy.

In 1976, under pressure from the federal government, the board of education adopted a plan to desegregate schools by making several schools magnet and specialty schools in a voluntary program. It was not successful, and the flight to the suburbs, along with the formation of charter schools, made matters worse.

With the sharp falloff in student enrollment, many schools closed. Kennedy School closed in 1977, and students transferred to Homedale. Development of River Village in the Doyle urban renewal area led to the redevelopment of Doyle School, replacing a later addition with new construction while preserving the original 1902 building when the new Doyle-Ryder School opened in 1981. In 1982, Stevenson School closed and was sold to Hurley Medical Center and torn down. Lowell Junior High abandoned the former Lewis School, which became Mott Adult High School's Lewis Center, which closed in 1987. Zimmerman Junior High closed in 1984 and became Mott Adult High School's Zimmerman Center, which closed in 2013.

The drop in enrollment in 1988 led to the closings of Bryant and Lowell Junior Highs, as well as Cummings, Jefferson, Lincoln, Walker and Selby Schools. Dewey School closed in 1991. Cook, Johnson, Martin and Pierson Schools were closed in 2002. Martin and Pierson students were moved to the old Bryant Junior High, which had served as Mott Adult High School's Bryant Center and became Bryant Elementary. In 2003, Cody, Homedale, Lawndale Avenue, Manley and Sobey Elementary Schools closed, as well as the Lowell Accelerated Academics Academy, which from 1990 to 1997 served the private Valley School.

Longfellow Junior High and King Elementary closed in 2006, followed by Whittier Classical Academy in the old junior high building, plus Cummings and Gundry Schools in 2008. Five elementary schools closed in 2009, Anderson, Civic Park, Garfield, Merrill and Stewart Schools, as well as the aging Central High. Two more elementary schools closed in 2010, Wilkins and Williams. Coolidge School closed in 2011, and students moved to the reopened Cummings School. McKinley Junior High, along with elementary schools Bunche and Summerfield, closed in 2012.

Northern High, as well as Bryant, Dort and Washington Schools, closed in 2013. Carpenter Road and Cummings Schools closed in 2015.

Scott Community School closed in 2016 but reopened in 2018 as the Flint Community Schools' Accelerated Learning Academy, serving seventh through twelfth grades. Northwestern High closed in 2018 and was converted to Flint Junior High School, which closed in 2020.

Lost Hospitals

At Flint's peak, it had six hospitals in the city, the centrally located Hurley Medical Center; St. Joseph Hospital, serving the east side; Flint General Hospital, serving the north side and McLaren General Hospital; Flint Osteopathic Hospital; and Genesee Memorial Hospital, serving the west side. But with the area's population loss starting in the 1980s, state officials wanted hospital bed capacity in the area to be reduced. St. Joseph Health Systems, which became Genesys Health Systems (now part of Ascension), took the lead in hospital consolidation in the Flint area beginning in 1982.

In 1921, the Sisters of St. Joseph founded St. Joseph Hospital, a Catholic hospital in the former home of Thomas Stockton on Ann Arbor Street. With expansions to the rear of the former home, that hospital outgrew the house and moved into its long-time location on Kensington Avenue in 1936. St. Joseph expanded over the years, including adding a nursing school in 1951. In 1992, St. Joseph Health Systems was renamed Genesys Health Systems, and the hospital was renamed Genesys Regional Medical Center–St. Joseph Campus. With the announcement in 1993 of plans for a new hospital, nursing home and health club in Grand Blanc Township, St. Joseph suspended its hospital replacement program and returned $2 million in donations the following year. In 1997, it closed with the opening of the new Genesys Health Park. The old hospital was torn down in 2000 to make way for the Mott Community College Regional Technology Center.

In May 1935, Dr. A.J. Still founded Flint Osteopathic Hospital (FOH) as a five-bed facility on Detroit Street (now Martin Luther King Avenue). In the 1940s, it moved to 416 West Fourth Avenue with eighteen beds. By 1955, it had increased its bed capacity, and the first board of trustees was appointed by the community at large. It began raising funds to build a new hospital at the corner of Beecher Road and Ballenger Highway, which opened in 1960. In 1988, it affiliated with St. Joseph Hospital and St. Joseph

The old Flint Osteopathic Hospital during demolition. *Gary Flinn.*

Health Systems. St. Joseph and Flint Osteopathic combined purchasing and warehousing in 1989. When St. Joseph Health Systems was renamed Genesys Health Systems, FOH became Genesys Regional Medical Center–Flint Osteopathic Campus in 1992. It closed in 1997 with the opening of the aforementioned Genesys Health Park. In 2014, McLaren Health System bought the empty hospital and tore it down the following year, determining that it was functionally obsolete. It remains a vacant lot, with McLaren using the old parking lot as overflow parking in 2020.

Flint General Hospital was an osteopathic hospital, established around 1938, located at 765 East Hamilton Avenue at North Street. In 1981, Kensington Health Systems (renamed St. Joseph Health Systems the following year) took over management of the ailing hospital. Renamed Family Hospital, it closed due to financial troubles in 1983. The closing of that hospital led to the formation of Hamilton Community Health Network, initially located inside the former hospital. It continues to serve the Flint area's low-income population. The former hospital is now New Paths, a substance abuse treatment center and halfway house.

Genesee Memorial Hospital opened in 1950 as the Genesee County Tuberculosis Sanitarium and by 1964 was renamed Genesee Memorial

Hospital. Originally controlled by Genesee County, it broke out on its own in 1986. In 1988, facing financial problems, it affiliated with St. Joseph Health Systems. With the formation of Genesys, it became Genesys Regional Medical Center–Genesee Memorial Campus. It closed in 1997 when Genesys Regional Medical Center opened in Grand Blanc Township. Genesee Memorial was torn down in 1999. It became green space on Ballenger Highway behind the McLaren MRI diagnostic center.

Lost Houses of Worship

Notable Protestant Churches

Because of the large number of Protestant churches and denominations that are and were in the city of Flint, this list is limited to the more notable churches that anchored neighborhoods. My apology in advance if a notable church that you believe should be included is not mentioned. The rules for inclusion were that the churches should be closed, consolidated or downsized. Active churches that moved to the suburbs are not included.

These are listed in the order that the landmark still-standing nineteenth-century downtown churches were built. They are St. Paul's Episcopal Church, built in 1872; First Presbyterian, built in 1885; and Court Street United Methodist (originally First Methodist Episcopal Church), built in 1893. As Flint grew in the twentieth century, additional churches were organized to serve the neighborhoods.

Episcopal Churches

Along with St. Paul's Episcopal, there were two other Episcopal churches in the city of Flint. Of the two, only St. Andrew's Episcopal on Iowa Street in Flint's Old East Side is still around. Sadly, Christ Episcopal at 322 East Hamilton Avenue, serving the north side, closed its doors, due to falling membership and demographic changes in the area. In 1988, the Christ Enrichment Center (now the Community Enrichment Center) was formed to provide enrichment opportunities and connections to services for youth and families in the former Christ Episcopal Church.

Presbyterian Churches

Besides what congregants affectionately call "First Pres," six other Presbyterian churches were organized in the city of Flint. None of them are Presbyterian churches now, as they were either consolidated or members moved to suburban Presbyterian churches in Flint Township, Davison, Mount Morris or Flushing. In 2007, Trinity Presbyterian Church on Lennon Road in Flint Township absorbed the congregations of Bethany and Christ the Liberator Presbyterian Churches. The former Bethany Presbyterian, at 1709 Nebraska, was sold in 2008 to Grace Cathedral Community Church. The former Christ the Liberator Presbyterian Church at 6202 Dupont Street is now Church Without Walls. The former Community Presbyterian Church at 2505 North Chevrolet Avenue is now the nondenominational Joy Tabernacle, which moved there in 2009. The former Fleming Road Presbyterian Church at 3918 Fleming Road currently houses the Prayer Garden Church of God in Christ. The former Parkland Presbyterian at 2001 West Carpenter Road is now Living Word Ministry. Sadly, the former Westminster Presbyterian Church at 2316 Corunna Road, which closed in 2007, is vacant and for sale. The asking price as of 2020 was $325,000. The real estate agent listed it as-is and offered a $2,500-per-month lease.

United Methodist Churches

Along with Court Street United Methodist Church downtown, there were eleven other United Methodist churches serving Flint neighborhoods. Of those, only three remain, Asbury UMC on Davison Road in the Old East Side and two west side UMC churches, Calvary on Flushing Road and Bethel on North Ballenger Highway.

Closed were the Central, Eastwood, Flint Park, Grace, Lincoln Park, Oak Park, St. James and Trinity UMC churches. The old Trinity UMC at 2200 Forest Hill Avenue is now Saints of God Church. The former Eastwood UMC at 3312 Whitter Avenue is now Mission of Peace Pentecostal Temple. Central UMC at 1309 North Ballenger Highway closed in 2004, with Bethel UMC moving there from 412 East Twelfth Street. The former Bethel UMC on Twelfth Street is now Church of Trinity Pentecostal. The old Flint Park Methodist Church at 106 East Flint Park Boulevard is now Evergreen Missionary Baptist Church. The former Grace UMC at 6009 North Saginaw Street is now Upper Room Missionary Baptist Church. The old Lincoln

The former Oak Park United Methodist Church. *Gary Flinn.*

Park UMC at 3410 Fenton Road closed in 2017 but currently operates as the South End Soup Kitchen. The former Oak Park UMC at 2125 North Saginaw was built in 1915 and closed in 2001. It was sold in 2007, becoming Freedom Center North, which closed in 2015 and is now vacant. Finally, St. James Methodist at 1144 Campau was wiped out by I-475 and the St. John urban renewal project.

Congregational Church

The First Congregational Church dates to 1867 as an outgrowth of the Presbyterian Church. The building at 215 West First Street (between Beach and Church) was dedicated free of debt in 1901. A fire destroyed the building in 1927. It was rebuilt in 1930. Around 1942, the church moved from the West First Street address to a new church at 803 Clifford Street as the First Congregational Unitarian Church. The old church was sold to the Flint Institute of Arts, which used it until the late 1950s. That building was then torn down to provide parking for the nearby telephone company workers. A split in this congregation in 1957 led to the Congregationalists (part of the merged United Church of Christ) joining First Baptist Church, which became the interdenominational Woodside Church. The Unitarians stayed on at the Clifford Street address as the

The First Congregational Church, which evolved into the now defunct Cross Congregational Church. *Author's collection.*

Unitarian Church of Flint, which moved around 1961 to the present South Ballenger Highway address in Flint Township. The old location on what is now Wallenberg Street is now a parking lot. The more conservative Congregationalists established the Cross Congregational Church at 1902 Sonny Avenue, which moved to Flint Township on Calkins Road in 1979 and dissolved in 2009. The old location on Sonny Avenue is now Blackwell AME Zion Church, founded in 1879, which was formerly located at 1234 Central in the old St. John Street area and was forced to move due to urban renewal.

Lutheran Churches

As Flint developed a more diverse population with more people of German heritage living in the city, St. Paul Lutheran Church was founded. Its second home was dedicated in 1918 at the corner of North Saginaw and Mary Streets. In 1960, it moved to its present location on South Ballenger Highway after the Flint Community Schools bought the old church, which was razed. With the decline of Flint's population, four notable Flint Lutheran churches either closed or were consolidated. Mount Olive Lutheran at 1819 Welch Boulevard consolidated with another Lutheran church in Flint Township.

That church on Welch is now Evangelistic Temple. The old Holy Trinity Lutheran at 109 Welch is now Mount Tabor Missionary Baptist Church. Redeemer Lutheran at 460 West Atherton is now Word of Life Christian Church. Calvary Lutheran at 2210 North Franklin is now the Franklin Avenue Mission.

Woodside Church on East Court Street

One of Flint's oldest congregations was organized in 1853 as the First Baptist Church. Before the Civil War, it was a stop on the Underground Railroad. Its first permanent home was at the corner of First Avenue and Lyon Street, and a Michigan Historical Marker shows where it stood. In 1890, its second permanent location was built at the southeast corner of Beach and Second Streets. It moved in 1952 to its landmark location at 1509 East Court Street, designed by world renowned Finnish architect Eero Saarinen and built by his brother-in-law Robert F. Swanson. The old location was torn down afterward and is now a parking lot.

The 1956–57 merger of the Congregational Christian Churches and the Evangelical & Reformed Church, forming the United Church of Christ, created a split among members of the First Congregational Unitarian Church. The Congregationalists left that church, and the remaining Unitarians renamed the church the Unitarian Church of Flint. First Baptist Church, a member of American Baptist Churches USA, joined United Church of Christ, becoming interdenominational, and invited Congregationalists to join in 1956. Because of the new interdenominational makeup of the congregation, it was renamed Woodside Church in 1961. Woodside Church is also affiliated with the Alliance of Baptists.

By 2016, Woodside Church membership was about 120 members with an attendance of about 70 on Sundays in a church designed for a congregation of 600 or more people. That, along with increasing maintenance for a church building more than sixty years old, led the congregation to put the building up for sale. It was sold to next door neighbor Mott Community College the following year. The church was renovated and became the Lenore Crowdy Family Life Center.

Woodside Church acquired and moved into an equally historic former automotive garage built in 1930 at 503 Garland Street in the historic Carriage Town area not far from its original permanent home.

The former Woodside Church on East Court Street. *Gary Flinn.*

Additional Baptist Churches

Additional Baptist churches of various denominations that are lost include First General Baptist Church, located at 1102 West Hemphill Road. That is now Christ the Rock Apostolic Church. Another Baptist congregation took over Shelton Heights Baptist Church, which is now New Community Baptist Church. The landmark Third Avenue Baptist Church at what is now 1114 University Avenue is now the Greater Flint Outreach Center.

Wesleyan Churches

While the city of Flint still has the First Flint Wesleyan Church on Davison Road in the northeast side of town, two other Wesleyan churches are lost. They are Brown Street Wesleyan at 2901 Brown Street, which is now Adoni International Ministries, and Chevrolet Avenue Wesleyan at 1352 North Chevrolet, which is now House of Solomon Apostolic Church.

First Church of the Nazarene/St. James CME Church

In 1924, the First Church of the Nazarene was founded by congregants who broke away from Central Church of the Nazarene and established their church at the corner of Lyon and Wood Streets. The groundbreaking for the new church took place on October 11 of that year, and the first service was held in the basement auditorium on December 14. The upper structure was added and dedicated on December 14, 1927. In the early 1950s, the split-level church was greatly enlarged, with the completion service held on February 17, 1952. The church at 1503 Lyon Street has its main sanctuary upstairs, with a sloping floor to the altar and featuring a long vestibule for crying babies. Downstairs were Sunday school classrooms, a small chapel and a social hall. By 1970, it had moved to a new church in Flint Township on Beecher Road. In 2012, with its membership down to around fifty people, the congregation dissolved, and members moved on to other churches. The Beecher Road church was sold and is now Victorious Word Church. The old church on Lyon Street became St. James Christian Methodist Episcopal Church. That church moved in 2011 to West Pierson Road in Mount Morris Township and closed in 2015. The church on Lyon Street has been deteriorating ever since.

Other Notable Lost Protestant Churches

Other lost Protestant Churches nominated by readers of my books' Facebook page are the West Flint Church of God at 1013 Hughes Avenue, which is now Calvary Apostolic Tabernacle; Oak Street Free Methodist Church at 718 Oak Street, which is now the Flint Odyssey House Recovery Chapel & Activity Center; and the Hungarian Reformed Church at 1829 Delaware Avenue, which is now Eastside Church of the Nazarene.

Lost Catholic Churches

The origin of Flint's Catholic community predates the city of Flint's founding in 1855. Flint's first schoolteacher was Daniel O' Sullivan, who arrived in 1834. He cofounded Flint's first Catholic church, St. Michael, built in 1844 at the corner of North Saginaw Street and Fifth Avenue. As

The First Church of the Nazarene during expansion, circa 1951. *Courtesy of Anthony Morey.*

The abandoned former First Church of the Nazarene, which was later St. James. CME. Church. *Gary Flinn.*

the city grew, that first church was replaced by a larger one in 1883, which is considered lost to disaster, as it was destroyed by fire in 1924. It was rebuilt the same year. That structure was torn down and replaced by the present church, which opened in 1966.

As the city grew, additional Catholic churches were organized and built, including All Saints' on Industrial Avenue near the Buick factory on the north side, in 1910; St. Matthew downtown, in 1911; St. Mary on what is now Franklin Avenue on the east side, in 1918; St. Joseph Hungarian on Hickory Street in the St. John Street area, in 1921; Sacred Heart on Stewart Avenue on the north side, in 1926; St. Agnes on West Pierson Road on the northwest side in 1928; Christ the King serving Flint's black Catholic community was formed in 1929 with the church built on Clifford Street south of downtown; St. John Vianney in the Mott Park neighborhood on Chevrolet and Blair, in 1940; and St. Luke on Forest Hill Avenue on Flint's northwest side, in 1950.

All Saints' was sold to Buick in 1956, and the church moved to Pierson Road in Mount Morris Township in 1958. One more new Catholic church opened, serving Flint's northeast side, St. Leo the Great on Wyoming Avenue in 1958.

One other church was lost to progress when Christ the King was forced to move in 1969 because it was in the path of the I-475 expressway. The new church at the corner of Seymour Avenue and Lapeer Road opened in 1972. A larger church later opened across Seymour.

By 1970, the city of Flint had ten Catholic churches. The St. John Street urban renewal project doomed St. Joseph Hungarian Catholic Church. It was torn down in 1973. Its congregants were absorbed by Blessed Sacrament in Burton, where a parish hall and rectory were built in memory of St. Joseph Hungarian, using funds from the closed church.

The White flight to the suburbs that began in the 1970s, along with General Motors factory closings in the 1980s, reduced the population of local Catholics, so the consolidation of Catholic churches was inevitable. Three Catholic churches, St. Luke, Sacred Heart and St. Agnes, were closed and consolidated in 2008. They absorbed by St. John Vianney. St. Leo closed in 2009, and Holy Rosary in Genesee Township absorbed the congregants. All Saints' closed in 2016, and the congregants absorbed into St. John Vianney. St. John Vianney also absorbed the congregants of Flint's oldest Catholic church, St. Michael, which closed in 2020.

As for what became of the closed former Catholic churches, Sacred Heart was razed, but the remaining building in the complex, the former

A portion of the abandoned St. Agnes Catholic Church and School campus. *Gary Flinn.*

Father Blasko Hall, is now the North End Soup Kitchen. St. Luke is now the St. Luke N.E.W. Life Center. St. Leo is now Agape Church of God in Christ. All Saints' on Pierson Road is now Reaching the World Ministries International. St. Michael was acquired by Catholic Charities of Shiawassee and Genesee Counties in 2021. Sadly, St. Agnes on Pierson Road is vacant and deteriorating.

Of the Catholic schools connected with churches in the city of Flint, only the St. John Vianney School on Bagley Street in Mott Park remains as the city of Flint's Catholic elementary school, along with Powers Catholic High School located on West Court Street in historic Fay Hall, built for the Michigan School for the Deaf. The old St. Mary School on Franklin Avenue was closed in 1992 and demolished in 2015. The closed and deteriorating St. Agnes School was last used as the Father DuKette Catholic School, which closed in 2008. St. Matthew School closed in 1970 when Powers Catholic opened. It later served as home of Valley School and then Alpha Montessori but then stood vacant for a number of years before it was demolished in 2008. St. Michael School also closed when Powers opened. It was leased to Flint Board of Education and became the School of Choice. After it left, Catholic Charities of Shiawassee and Genesee Counties took it over, and it became Sister Claudia Burke Center for Hope. The former school was partially demolished in 2017, with the remaining portion remodeled with a new entrance.

Temple Beth El on Liberty Street, where I-475 is now. *Courtesy of Temple Beth El.*

Lost Synagogues

The Jewish population in Flint was slow in developing. The first Jewish resident settled in 1859. By the 1870s, a small cluster of Jewish families lived in Flint until the early 1900s. The number was too small for Jewish activities outside homes. Most made their living as storekeepers or peddlers. The first notable Jewish resident to establish strong roots was Harry Winegarden, who moved to Flint in 1895 and founded the New Orleans Fruit House. He became a prominent Flint citizen, with later generations living in the area even today.

The growth of Flint's automotive industry also led to new diversity in Flint's population, and by 1920, there were a sufficient number of Jewish residents to establish a synagogue. Congregation Beth Israel on McFarlan Street opened in 1921. By 1927, Jewish residents who practiced Reform Judaism, including Harry Winegarden, established Temple Beth El. Ten years later, it opened a permanent home in a former private residence at the corner of Liberty and East Second Streets.

After World War II, the increasing number of member families and their children forced Congregation Beth Israel and Temple Beth El to build new facilities, which both opened in 1950. Beth Israel built a large synagogue on Flint's north side at the corner of Hamilton Avenue and Oren Street. Beth

El built its temple on Flint's west side at the corner of Ballenger Highway and Beecher Road.

As for the former locations, Temple Beth El became St. Nicholas Orthodox Church. But the old house at 521 Liberty Street was in the path of the I-475 expressway, and the church was forced to move in 1970 to its new location on Center Road in Burton. It was torn down by 1971. The former Congregation Beth Israel at 735 McFarlan Street became the Lebanon Community Center until around 1970. It was briefly the King's Hall African Age & Cultural Center but fell victim to the Doyle urban renewal project and was gone by 1974.

By the 1970s, demographic changes and a lack of parking forced Beth Israel to move. It was sold to Christ Fellowship Baptist Church, which still uses it today. Congregation Beth Israel moved to Flint Township and a larger synagogue at the corner of Calkins and Dye Roads.

The Flint area's Jewish population peaked in the 1970s and began to decline. With the gradual decline of the automotive industry, many younger Flint Jews left the area to pursue employment opportunities elsewhere. With fewer children attending separate Hebrew schools at Beth El and Beth Israel, the congregations merged the schools in 1982, thereby creating the Ivriah, a combined Hebrew school subsidized by both congregations and the Flint Jewish Federation.

As Temple Beth El was nearing fifty years old in the 1990s, it had become a maintenance headache, requiring thousands of dollars just to keep it in repair. So, when McLaren Hospital across Beecher Road expressed an interest in purchasing the building, a committee was organized to design

Temple Beth El on Ballenger Highway, where the McLaren Endoscopy and Imaging Center is now. *Courtesy of Temple Beth El.*

and build a smaller and more manageable temple. This temple then opened in 1998 on Calkins Road in Flint Township, next door to Congregation Beth Israel. The former temple was briefly used by McLaren for educational classes before it was razed in 2005. The McLaren Endoscopy and Imaging Center now occupies the former site.

As membership at Congregation Beth Israel declined when members died or moved away, the Calkins Road synagogue, built in 1972, was becoming more expensive to maintain. So, in 2016, it was sold and became the Genesee STEM Academy, a charter school. After holding services in an office building on Miller Road for a couple of years, it made arrangements with Temple Beth El to share its synagogue building in 2018. The Temple Beth El library was converted into a small chapel for Beth Israel to hold services.

LOST COMMERCIAL STRIPS

In 1953, the National Civic League awarded Flint the designation of an All-America City, based on the area's quick response to the tornado that devastated the Beecher Metropolitan District north of the city. The 1950s were a booming time for the city, which saw commercial development of neighborhoods, drawing commerce away from downtown. But as commercial development shifted from one commercial center to another, later moving to suburban areas, previous developments started to deteriorate or become abandoned. Two commercial strips in different parts of Flint extending outside the city are notable examples.

Clio Road

The Clio Road commercial strip developed from south of Pasadena Avenue northward to include Mount Morris Township. The completion of the Northwest Shopping Center (now Hallwood Plaza) in 1957 at the corner of Clio and Pierson Roads helped to push development of the Clio Road strip. It was built by Hamady Bros. Food Markets, an anchor store, along with the then supermarket sized Yankee Store, which in 1961, was replaced by the first Yankee Stadium full-sized department store, the first addition to that shopping center. Later in the 1960s, the Fair was built to complete the Clio Road side of the shopping center as the second department store anchor.

Clio Road north of Pierson Road also developed into an automobile row with new car dealerships extending northward to Mount Morris Road. The strip began with a Ford dealership at 5510 Clio Road, then a Lincoln-Mercury (later Toyota) dealership at G-4205 Clio Road, then a Chrysler-Plymouth-Dodge dealer at 5928 Clio Road, a Buick dealership at G-4315 Clio Road, a Chevrolet dealership at G-5100 Clio Road next to a Buick dealership that went bankrupt at G-5200 Clio Road and farther north between Stanley and Mount Morris Roads, a Pontiac-Oldsmobile dealership at G-7401 Clio Road. Of all those new car dealerships, only the Chevrolet dealer remains on Clio Road. The other dealerships either closed or moved to another location. The Mercury, Plymouth, Pontiac and Oldsmobile brands were orphaned. The nearest Ford dealer is in Flushing. The Chrysler-Dodge and Toyota dealerships are now in Grand Blanc. The Buick dealer is in Flint Township. As of early 2021, the Flint area does not have a Lincoln dealership.

Along with the large department stores in the Northwest Shopping Center, there were also Arlan's on Pierson and Clio Roads and Woolco in the Mayfair Plaza at G-4401 Clio Road in Mount Morris Township. The Mayfair plaza also had an A&P (later Mansour) supermarket. Next to Arlan's was a Wrigley/Big Valu/Packer/Vescio supermarket. Kroger was on Clio near Pasadena. Robert Hall Clothes was another notable retail presence, and when it closed when Robert Hall Village moved into the Yankee space, Grapevine Records moved in.

Clio Road boasted two bowling alleys, West Lanes at 5409 Clio Road and Northwest Bowl at G-4359 Clio Road, as well as a health club and the Farm Motel, which had a tavern and restaurant. The Clio Road strip was best known for its abundance of restaurants, both local and national, starting with the McDonald's on Clio and Pasadena. Dawn Donuts became a landmark at the same intersection. The very first Arby's serving Flint was there. Others included Taco Bell, KFC, the Hungry Penguin, Pizza Hut, Chick-N-Joy, Burger King, London Guard Fish & Chips, Sveden House and Farrell's Ice Cream Parlor. Local eateries included the Texan, Palace Pizzeria, the Pink Garter Steak House, the PX Bar-B-Q and the Golden Point. Of course, the big hangout on Clio and Pierson Roads was the A&W Drive-in and farther north was Herriman's Dairy. Among the bars and cocktail lounges were O'Toole's, the Golden Nugget Saloon across from the Northwest Shopping Center (on Pierson Road), the Good Times Bar and the Track.

This page, top: Dawn Donuts on Clio Road and Pasadena Avenue. The landmark sign is original but not the building, which was replaced in recent years. *Gary Flinn*

This page, bottom: Former Hungry Penguin on Clio Road. *Gary Flinn.*

Opposite, top: The Farm Motel on Clio Road. *Author's collection.*

Opposite, bottom: What's left of the former Farm Motel and Restaurant. *Gary Flinn.*

There were numerous other businesses on Clio Road. But when the Genesee Valley Shopping Center was built in 1970 on Miller and Linden Roads, commerce gradually shifted to Flint Township and many of the above businesses either closed or moved. You can still see signs of Clio Road's heyday, including old signs still in place for Palace Pizzeria and the Hungry Penguin.

At the Hallwood Plaza, the Fair store space that was vacant since March 1989 was torn down by the start of 1997 because of high maintenance costs

Top: The former Top Hat Auto Wash on Clio Road. *Gary Flinn.*

Bottom: The former Kroger Store on Pierson and Clio Roads in the Hallwood Plaza, formerly the Northwest Shopping Center. It was built as a Yankee Stadium department store. After Kroger closed, it was briefly an unsuccessful revival of a Hamady supermarket. *Gary Flinn.*

for the vacant two-story space. A free-standing Huntington Bank branch now occupies the space. The former Yankee Stadium Store anchor space had a few successor tenants over the years but became vacant after an attempted revival of the Hamady supermarket closed in 2018, less than four months after opening.

Dort Highway

In 1923, on what was then Western Road, the Dort Motor Company built a factory that later became AC Spark Plug. In 1926–27, the state constructed a bypass road to relieve congestion downtown, which the city named Dort Highway. Commercial development slowly developed around the factory. In the 1950s, two new car dealerships were built along South Dort Highway, the company-owned East Side Buick and independent dealer Superior Pontiac-Cadillac. Commercial development of South Dort Highway south of the factory began to develop with the post–World War II boom. In 1946, the Dort Drive-in Theatre, Flint's first drive-in, was built at the corner of South Dort Highway and Atherton Road. In 1948, Hamady Bros. Food Markets opened its distribution warehouse and flagship supermarket on South Dort Highway.

As Flint grew in the 1950s, there was more commercial development. Winegarden Furniture built a new store next to the drive-in. Across the street was a Royal Drive-in restaurant. At the start of South Dort Highway, a Kroger store was built. The Blossom Shoppe Garden Center was at Dort and Court. A fine-dining restaurant south of Court Street was the Shorthorn. One notable business south of Lapeer Road was Clark's Store Fixtures, notable for its kitchen supplies. Robert Hall had a store near Lippincott. GMC Quality Truck Sales was another automotive dealership. Other eateries included the Bell Tone, Bill Knapp's, Howard Johnson's, Nino's, Mr. Steak, Sveden House, Superior Coney Island, Pizza Hut, Bonanza Steakhouse, Lum's, Trevi's Pizzeria, the Pancake House, American Grill and El Rancho. Watering holes included the Stables, the Aloha Lounge (the Trade Winds), Gaslight Inn, Contos, the Patio Lounge, the Empire Lounge, Tony's Cocktails, the Embers, JB's Lounge and the Palace Garden. Other notable businesses included Pier 1 Imports, TV Engineers, Frank's Nursery & Crafts and a few mobile home dealerships.

When the Dort Mall was built in the mid-1960s where the drive-in theater once stood, with the Yankee Stadium store as its main anchor, a Kmart store was built south of the mall. South Dort Highway boasted three bowling alleys, Panorama Lanes, the Eastown Bowl and the Dort Bowl. There were also two movie theaters, the Flint Cinema and the Dort Mall Cinema, along with a health spa.

Later called the Small Mall, the Dort Mall had a drugstore with adjacent restaurant, along with a Harbor House cafeteria in the former A&P supermarket space, which briefly housed Circus Time Pizza in the 1980s.

Top: Former Bill Knapp's on Dort Highway. *Gary Flinn.*

Bottom: The former Superior Pontiac-Cadillac on Dort Highway. *Gary Flinn.*

The mall also had Friar Tuck's. The basement contained a disco called the Light in the 1970s and 1980s.

South Dort Highway started going downhill when, in 1977, another movie theater opened but not the kind of theater to take the family to, as the Cinema Blue showed porn. When the Eastland Mall (now Courtland Center) opened in Burton on Court Street and Center Road, commerce

Top: A mostly vacant commercial strip on South Dort Highway, which included the long gone Winegarden Furniture. *Gary Flinn.*

Bottom: A former Walgreens on Dort Highway and Atherton Road. *Gary Flinn.*

gradually shifted to Center Road, especially after Meijer opened a store on Center Road near Atherton in Burton. None of the mentioned businesses on Dort Highway are there anymore, including the porn theater, which is now the Deja Vu strip club.

North Dort Highway was anchored by the AC Spark Plug factory complex, which sparked such commercial developments as the A&P supermarket and

Top: The former Cinema Blue on Dort Highway. *Gary Flinn.*

Bottom: The former Kmart on Dort Highway. *Gary Flinn.*

warehouse, Arlan's department store, Dining World and numerous bars and restaurants, including Nite Owl Coney Island, the Doll House, Kelush's Bar, Deno's Lounge, Mavis Cocktail Lounge, the Stables, Aunt Nina's, the Gross Point Inn, Sandy's Pizza and Lee's Famous Recipe.

LOST TO NEGLECT

Windmill Place

Windmill Place was one result of the Doyle urban renewal project at the corner of North Saginaw Street and Fifth Avenue. It was a four-building complex featuring commercial businesses, offices and a food court. Building A was built to house fifteen eateries and a few specialty shops. Building B housed the Courtside Restaurant and a bar. Building C was connected to B by an enclosed walkway to house retail space. Building D was planned to house a pharmacy and supermarket but wound up housing offices. There was also the Electric Avenue Arcade.

Among the eateries initially located in Windmill Place were Aida's Midwestern Food, Anna's Kitchen, the Captain's Galley, Costa's Coney Island, Fisher Bar-B-Q, the Hungarian Gourmet, Jack's Deli, Moy Kong Express, the Potato Patch, Ruggero's and That Salad Place. Various treats were offered by the Candy Shop, Cookie Tin, Farmer's Market Bakery and Stroh's Ice Cream & Yogurt.

Businesses were served by American Speedy Print, Citizens Bank and Superior Travel. Retail shops included Computer Portraits by B&D, Island Treasures, Rollie Pollies, the Smoke Shop and Take Five. Style Inn offered hair styling and manicures. Entertainment was offered by Invaders 2 video arcade. A co-op of artists operated the Artists Studio in Building A.

It was one of a few attempts at downtown Flint development, including Water Street Pavilion and AutoWorld. As earlier noted, Water Street Pavilion was taken over by the University of Michigan–Flint and became University Pavilion. AutoWorld was demolished and is now part of the UM–Flint campus, with the White Building constructed on the former site. Windmill Place closed at the same time AutoWorld closed. Businessman Don Williamson, who became Flint mayor, bought Windmill Place in 1988.

It was sold in 1995 to a religious group that formed the Metropolitan Housing Development Corporation. The tenants left one by one, and an organization called AEV Inc. took over management of the complex. The two-story Building A was torn down in 2007 because of interior damage due to a leaky roof and to make way for a Family Dollar store, which required additional parking.

In 2011, AEV fell behind on its property taxes and has closed its real estate office in the complex, which now lists 877 5th LLC as the owner of

Windmill Place shortly before demolition. *Gary Flinn.*

the property on Flint property tax records. The new owner, 877 5th LLC, is located inside the Mott Foundation Building.

Today, only the Family Dollar store is standing. When this writer first visited the site on May 1, the remaining Windmill Place buildings were boarded up. Pictures were not taken until later because of police tape around the driveway. That was because a security guard at Family Dollar was shot and killed by a man who was refused entry during the COVID-19 pandemic because he was not wearing a face mask. In August 2020, the remaining Windmill Place buildings were torn down.

North and South Flint Plazas

In 1953, the Taubman Company, which over the years has built numerous regional shopping malls, built its first shopping center, the North Flint Plaza, at the corner of West Pierson Road at Detroit Street (now Martin Luther King Avenue), opened in 1954. Federal Department Store, a Kroger supermarket and a Kresge variety store served as its anchor stores. In 1956, Taubman built the South Flint Plaza, which was an even larger open-air shopping center on Fenton Road at Hemphill Road just outside Flint's city limits in what was then Burton Township. The city would annex that shopping center from the township. Anchoring the South Flint Plaza were two department stores, Federal's and the Fair. A National Foods supermarket and Kresge's store also anchored the South Flint Plaza. A 1959 addition included Flint's first Montgomery Ward store.

Along with Federal's and Kresge's, which operated in both the North and South Flint Plaza, another retailer that operated in both shopping centers was Mill End dry goods. They were the first major shopping areas that shifted commerce away from downtown. Over the years, various smaller shops came and went in the two shopping centers. In the South Flint Plaza, there was a Little Caesars pizza restaurant, an Imperial Sports sporting goods store, a Rainbow USA clothing store, a Dollar Tree store, a Secretary of State branch office, Morrie's Furniture, a Genesee Bank (now Chase Bank), Citi Trends and Thal's, among other stores.

After Federal's filed for bankruptcy protection, it closed its three Flint area locations, including the North and South Flint Plaza, plus the Eastland Mall (now Courtland Center) in Burton in the early 1970s. Eventually, the former North Flint Plaza location was occupied by a Greenley's furniture warehouse. Greenley's already had a store in the South Flint Plaza. Greenley's offered hard goods, but that noted Flint area chain closed in 1985. The North Flint Plaza space became vacant from that point onward. The South Flint Plaza location was taken over by the Woolco discount department store. That chain closed in 1983. Value City Furniture took over the South Flint Plaza space in the mid-1990s.

Montgomery Ward in the South Flint Plaza closed in 1974. Eventually, a Hamady supermarket moved from the former National Foods location into the old Wards location. After Hamady went out of business in 1991, a Save A Lot grocery store took over the space.

The Fair store in the South Flint Plaza closed in 1982. Two years later, Value City Department Store moved into that space.

McCrory in the South Flint Plaza closed in 1997, and an A.J. Wright store moved into the space in 2003.

In 2011, a Marshalls discount clothing store opened in the South Flint Plaza. Slow sales led to that store closing after only nine months.

The South Flint Plaza lost its anchor stores, with Value City Department Store closed in 2008, followed by Value City Furniture in 2015. Save A Lot closed afterward.

At the North Flint Plaza, after Kroger closed, Landmark Foods took over the space and continues to anchor that shopping center today. Other tenants by the 1990s were a Family Dollar store, a Genesee County Department of Social Services food stamp center, several smaller shops and a few vacant

Top: North Flint Plaza today. *Gary Flinn*

Bottom: South Flint Plaza today. *Gary Flinn.*

spaces. Among the tenants that disappeared by the mid-1990s were the Flint Public Library North Flint branch, Perfect Cleaners and Kopland Pharmacy. On December 19, 1995, fire broke out at the R&S Trading Post. Because fire fighters were hampered by security bars at the business, as well as low water pressure from the hydrants, the business was destroyed. For insurance purposes, the L side of the shopping center facing Martin Luther King Avenue was considered a total loss and that side, which included the vacant Federal's/Greenley's space, was torn down the following August. In 2019, the North Flint Plaza got a boost when the anchor space that Kresge's first occupied was taken over by the Oak Street Health Clinic.

On the other hand, the South Flint Plaza is now mostly vacant with only a 15 percent occupancy rate and was auctioned off in August 2020. Its future is uncertain.

Thompson's Shopping Center

In 1946, Thompson's Super Market opened at the corner of Richfield Road and Term Street on Flint's northeast side on the city limits. Genesee Township is across Richfield Road. Also on that strip was a Rexall drug store, a shoe store and a Ben Franklin store.

In 1965, an even larger shopping center was built with storefronts facing Richfield Road and Term Street with large parking areas in front of them. It was an example of googie architecture, which was popular at that time. It was topped off with multiple backlit oval letters mounted on high steel pylons with "THOMPSONS" on both sides of the storefronts.

For the grand opening, there was a crowd to see country singer Kenny Roberts, who at the time hosted a children's show on WNEM-TV5.

Simpson's Shoes and Richardson's Rexall Drugs moved out of the original strip into the new shopping center, allowing both Ben Franklin and Thompson's Super Market to absorb those spaces. The shoe store (later Morrie's) had a "shu-ranch" children's shoe department with a caged monkey and a funhouse mirror. Other tenants included the Peter Pan children's clothing store, Sperry's Jewelry, a State Farm Insurance agent, a dentist's office, a barber shop, Brown's Shoe Repair, Gail's Clip 'n Curl beauty salon, Jean Carol Fashions and the Norge Laundry Village.

In 1968, an addition to the east end of the shopping center facing Richfield Road was built as the new location of the Ben Franklin store. The supermarket took over most of the former Ben Franklin space with

Top: Thompson's Shopping Center as it looked circa 1967. *Courtesy of Diana Robere.*

Bottom: Fenced in and vacant Thompson's Shopping Center in 2020. *Gary Flinn.*

a Dad 'n Lad men's clothing store taking over the rest of the space. The drugstore, under new ownership, was renamed People's Drugs and moved into a larger addition next to Ben Franklin. That drugstore would later become Cook's Drugs and then Perry Drugs.

Over the years, the mix of stores would change. The laundromat closed, and a Genesee Bank (later NBD) branch opened in the former space. A Radio Shack store and a flower shop moved in. The supermarket became Thompson's Cracker Barrel and then Mr. B's, followed by Plaza Food. In 1986, both shopping center buildings were extensively renovated, with all of the googie architectural details removed to create more contemporary storefronts.

When the last remaining store in the shopping center, a Family Dollar, vacated by 2017, it was completely vacant. The supermarket space was gutted by fire. In 2020, the entire shopping center space was fenced in, with its fate unknown.

The Decline of an Apartment Complex

Ballenger Manor Apartments consisted of three buildings with eleven units each, built in 1961 at the corner of Ballenger Highway and Westcombe Avenue on Flint's west side. At that time, it was considered to be ideal housing for people employed at three nearby hospitals, Flint Osteopathic Hospital, Genesee Memorial Hospital and McLaren General Hospital.

Genesee Memorial was built around 1950 as the Genesee County Tuberculosis Sanitarium and by 1964 was renamed Genesee Memorial Hospital. McLaren General Hospital was built in 1951 and was expanded three times in subsequent years. Flint Osteopathic Hospital was built in 1960. Genesee Memorial and Flint Osteopathic closed in 1997 when Genesys Regional Medical Center opened in Grand Blanc Township. Genesee Memorial was torn down in 1999. Flint Osteopathic was mainly empty and in 2014 was sold to McLaren. It was determined that the old hospital was functionally obsolete, so the old Flint Osteopathic Hospital was torn down in 2015, and the former site is vacant.

Ballenger Manor Apartments suffered a slow death, beginning with a fatal fire in 2013, which destroyed Building C and claimed the life of one resident. In 2016, the owners had trouble paying the water bill but managed to pay it at the last minute. But a major water leak in Building A in January 2017 forced the residents to find new housing. The rest of the residents moved out shortly afterward, after water service was cut off.

Suspected squatters started a fire that gutted Building A in 2018. Both Ballenger Manor buildings have been deteriorating ever since. In 2019, an unauthorized installation of roof shingles without the proper building permit took place on both buildings. The installation was shoddy, causing sections of the roof to blow off in high winds. Despite the renovation of the former Coolidge School into apartments, the eyesore that was the Ballenger

The abandoned Ballenger Manor Apartments. *Gary Flinn.*

Manor Apartments continue to be a blot on Flint's west side, along with other vacant buildings that continue to deteriorate. The fate of Ballenger Manor Apartments is still tied up in the courts. The neighborhood consensus calls for their demolition. While the buildings have been slated for demolition by the city, Genesee County circuit court judge Celeste Bell still has to decide the dispute between property owners about who gets the insurance money that would then be used to pay for demolition. The court case was still pending in early 2021.

LOST NEIGHBORHOODS

The Old East Side

The Old East Side on the northeast side of town is bounded by the Flint River to the north and west, Dort Highway to the east and Robert T. Longway Boulevard to the south. There were three commercial areas along Franklin Avenue, Davison Road and Lewis Street. The southwestern part of the area west of Lewis Street south of Davison Road was wiped out in the early 1970s to make way for I-475. Before TV came along, the Roxy Theatre on Broadway, east of Lewis, showed movies until it closed in 1957. It was torn down around 1971. Three elementary schools served the neighborhood, Homedale on Davison Road, built in 1913; Lewis on Franklin Avenue, built in 1917; and Washington on North Vernon Avenue, built in 1922. Next to Lewis School was Lowell Junior High, built in 1929, which, as mentioned, annexed Lewis in 1970. Lewis was replaced by Williams School, which also replaced the predominately Black Roosevelt School on the other side of the Flint River, a textbook example of integrating a Flint elementary school with the Flint Board of Education's history of past racism.

The blue-collar working-class neighborhood developed with the growth of the automotive industry at the start of the twentieth century. Restrictive covenants made it a predominately White neighborhood. But like the St. John Street neighborhood on the other side of the Flint River, the population included immigrants from Europe who came to work in the expanding automotive factories. A class distinction developed between the blue-collar people living north of Longway and the white-collar people living south of Longway. Among the surnames mentioned by former Old East Side residents were Abbot, Anderson, Butash, Campbell, Cole, Gilles, Medved, Mercier, Plamondon, Rodabough, Ruddy and Papp.

Across from Homedale School were storefronts. A chainsaw shop with an attached apartment was there, and a local landmark on the same block was Gypsy Jack's house with Old West memorabilia decorating the property. Not far from Lewis School on Franklin was the Trading Post market, which looked like a log trading post and had a cigar store Indian or a statue of a king. There was also a Ben Franklin Store on Franklin. A Lewis Street landmark that is still in operation is Knoblock Hardware. Hamady had a large supermarket on Davison and Franklin, which is now Fresh Choice Market Place.

Over time, the Old East Side became a mainly Latino community. With the decline of Flint's population in the 1980s and as older residents died, numerous vacant houses began to dot the area, and it became a magnet for arsonists by 2010, causing whole blocks in the area to become vacant lots. One Old East Side tragedy that hit this writer hard was when local radio host and owner of Helen's Records & Gifts on Franklin, Helen Gonzales, was murdered in 2005 in her shop by an undocumented immigrant wielding a hammer. That building is long gone. The vacant Homedale School burned down in 2010. The formerly vibrant commercial areas became vacant lots, especially on Franklin Avenue. The old Lewis School was torn down in 1988. The vacant Lowell Junior High School, plus Washington and Williams Elementary Schools, are deteriorating. Lowell looks the worst, as

Wendy All's grandparents' home on Leith Street near Franklin Avenue, now a vacant lot. Her grandfather Istvan "Steve" All was an upholsterer at Fisher Body. Her grandmother Mary Suhayda All was an inspector at AC Spark Plug. Mary's father, Istvan Suhayda, founded Suhayda Bros. Store located on St. John Street in Flint. *Courtesy of Wendy All.*

The corner of Franklin Avenue and Leith Street in the Old East Side in 2020. *Gary Flinn.*

its aluminum windows were stolen, and it shows scars from when military exercises were held there in 2015.

A major blow to the Old East Side came in 2018 when neighborhood landmark Angelo's Coney Island restaurant closed its flagship location on Davison Road and Franklin Avenue after nearly seventy years in operation.

Carriage Town

The founders of the Carriage Town Historic Neighborhood Association (CTHNA), established in 1982, boasted that it was Flint's first neighborhood. The neighborhood was established by Chauncey Payne as the Village of Grand Traverse. He drew a plat map in 1837, eighteen years before Flint became a city. Payne was married to Flint founder Jacob Smith's daughter Louisa. Smith's trading post was located near the Flint River, where the intersection of First Avenue and Lyon Street is now. The Carriage Town boundaries are Fifth Avenue to the north, North Saginaw Street to the east, Begole Street to the west and the Flint River to the south. Smith established his trading post there, doing business with the Chippewa Nation. Just east of present-day Atwood Stadium there is a fenced-in ancient Chippewa burial ground that was discovered in 2008. It was discovered during planned construction of new homes in a collaboration between the CTHNA and the Genesee County Land Bank. So, this area was first settled by the native Chippewa people.

The Carriage Town name came about because Flint became a leading carriage maker by the end of the nineteenth century. The Flint Road Cart Company, which evolved into the Durant-Dort Carriage Company, began in 1886 on Water Street (named South Street then) at the Flint River in a former woolen mill built six years before. The Durant-Dort Carriage Company's administration building was and is still across the street, and it was stated that it became the birthplace of General Motors when it was founded by Durant-Dort co-owner Billy Durant. The Durant-Dort office building, one of forty-two National Landmarks in Michigan, was restored by the Genesee County Historical Society at a cost of $1 million and now serves as the society's offices. The original factory building is now Factory One, which is owned by General Motors. With production of Durant-Dort carriages discontinued in 1917, the complex became the Dort Motor Car Company and began building automobiles in 1915. So, motorcar and horse-drawn carriage production did overlap for two years. Dort built a factory nearby at the corner of Grand Traverse and Water Street, which became Factory Two and now operates as a small business incubator.

The reason for the CTHNA's formation was to highlight the Carriage Town neighborhood's history as a leading producer of horse-drawn vehicles, giving Flint the nickname of the Vehicle City, and to promote the rehabilitation of historic homes, including the homes of carriage company workers and company management. At the time of the formation of the CTHNA, the area had the worst crime rate in the city, with drugs, crime, bad landlords and prostitution.

Doing everything possible to make Carriage Town a better place to live, the CTHNA collaborated with other nonprofits and had low interest loan programs for exterior work on homes, neighborhood beautification, marketing and a neighborhood design center.

But the efforts of restoration and rehabilitation have been mixed, with several setbacks. In 2010, the Jackson Hardy House, with a restored exterior and funding to restore the interior, and the vacant house next door on Garland Street were destroyed in a suspected arson fire. Today where the Jackson Hardy House once stood at the corner of Garland Street and University Avenue is a memorial with no markings.

Despite the pleas of preservationists, several blighted homes near Hurley Medical Center, located just north of Carriage Town, were demolished in 2015. Now there is green space where there used to be homes between Hurley Medical Center and Atwood Stadium.

A house that was built in 1910 and served from 1955 until 1997 as the House of Spencer Mortuary was left abandoned after it closed. Rumored to be haunted, the abandoned funeral home at 520 West University Avenue was turned into a center for the arts in 2012 by the Flint Public Art Project. But it was unexpectedly demolished in November 2018.

While several homes were restored in the area, a few others remain unrestored, and there are several vacant lots. Numerous dwellings are vacant, including the home where noted auto executive Charles W. Nash once lived on Mason Street. Nash was a Durant-Dort employee who was promoted to general manager, moved on to Buick and went on to become General Motors president before moving to Kenosha, Wisconsin, to start Nash Motors, which evolved into American Motors Corporation.

Kettering University has been doing its part in making improvements to the University Avenue Corridor. For example, it took over and made improvements to Atwood Stadium. It spearheaded the renaming of Third

Avenue to University Avenue to note that the street connects Kettering University with the University of Michigan–Flint.

Civic Park

Flint's rapid growth from the automotive industry led to plans for a new subdivision drawn up in 1917, called Civic Park, on land that was part of the Stockdale and Durant family farms. Like many real estate developments in Flint, deeds for houses at Civic Park contained the following for deed restriction no. 2, which forbid anyone who "is not wholly of the white or Caucasian race" to occupy the home. Planning a self-contained, self-sufficient Civic Park was as much about providing for its families as it was about keeping others out. As was stated earlier, such restrictive covenants were made illegal and unenforceable by laws at the local, state and national level in the 1960s. Roughly bounded by Begole Street to the south, Clio Road to the west, Dartmouth and Genesee Streets to the north and Dupont Street to the east, it was originally developed by the Civic Building Company, headed by William W. Mountain, general manager of Flint Varnish Works, and Jonathan E. Burroughs, who owned a flour mill, later led Citizens Bank and spearheaded development of the Flint Cultural Center. But material shortages brought about by World War I slowed development of the neighborhood. So, in 1919, General Motors founded Modern Housing Corporation as a GM subsidiary to deal with the housing shortage in Flint and other cities with GM factories in similar situations to avoid dealing with factory workers living in tents and tar-paper shacks. Modern Housing took over developing Civic Park, and a special Grand Trunk railroad line was built to send freight trains from the downtown depot every six minutes, twenty-four hours a day, carrying two thousand tons of material to the muddy fields where the neighborhood was developed.

To provide services for the builders, a work camp was created to accommodate 4,600 workers. There were 96 bunkhouses and two commissaries that could feed 1,500 at a single sitting. There were barbershops, shoe repair shops and several open-air theaters. Five sawmills cut hemlock and yellow pine around the clock. In the nine months between 1919 and 1920, GM built 950 houses of varying design on 280 acres of farmland, a notable achievement.

To serve the neighborhood, Civic Park School was built in 1922, and Haskell Community Center at Bassett Park was built in 1923. A commercial area on Dayton Place across from Civic Park School developed and featured small shops and a supermarket. The supermarket was originally Comber's Dayton Street Market at 1401 West Dayton Street. By 1974, it was Double D Supermarket and became Rico's Sav-On Foods in 1992, until it was destroyed by fire around 2003.

There's a larger commercial block at the southeast end bounded by Welch Boulevard, Mount Elliott Avenue, Stockdale Street and Chevrolet Avenue. Directly across Welch just outside Civic Park was additional commercial space that used to be anchored by the Della Theatre, which operated from 1937 until 1964, when Genesee Bank bought it and tore it down to make way for drive-through windows adjacent to the bank.

The White flight in northwest Flint, which caused major demographic changes in the area, resulted in a predominately Black population in the 1970s did not seriously affect Civic Park initially as the then diverse population, another term for racially integrated, continued to thrive at that time. Because Civic Park was among the earliest planned neighborhoods in the United States, it was listed in the National Register of Historic Places in 1979.

The 1980s job losses in Flint started to affect Civic Park as well. Increased poverty, crime and illegal drug availability took its toll. In an attempt to stem the tide of deterioration, the City of Flint and the C.S. Mott Foundation published the Civic Park Home Preservation Manual in 1981. It gave instructions on how to make repairs and home improvements to homes in the Civic Park neighborhood while retaining the homes' historical integrity. This included replacing worn out or deteriorated building material with identical material. While over the years, newer asbestos, aluminum or vinyl siding were installed in some houses, historic preservation calls for removal of such siding.

With the jobs gone, many of the workers who lived in Civic Park also left. Residents complained in 1985 about dope houses, the lack of housing code enforcement and road repairs from residents. More rental housing caused more deterioration as homes were neglected and then abandoned. Civic Park School closed in 2009, and to add insult to injury, its aluminum windows, which were installed after the school was gutted by fire in 1972, were stolen in 2011, so the openings were boarded up. The school is vacant and deteriorating. Funding issues made Haskell Community Center's future uncertain.

In 2013, Flint Area Reinvestment Office, with funding from the United Way and Diplomat Pharmacy, commissioned ICF International to perform a study of the Civic Park neighborhood. It determined that the "Civic Park Historic District no longer meets the criteria under which it

The Heritage and Harmony stage at Civic Park, where a supermarket used to stand. *Gary Flinn.*

was originally listed....This is due to the loss of historic integrity." Indeed, the makeup of Civic Park's housing stock showed in 2013 that 23 percent of historic properties retained their historic integrity and were occupied. The same percentage of historic properties also retained historic integrity but were not occupied. It stated that 21 percent of properties had no historic integrity and were unoccupied, 20 percent of properties had no historic integrity and were occupied and 13 percent of properties were vacant lots.

In 2018, the first Heritage & Harmony Festival was held on the vacant lot where the neighborhood supermarket once stood across from Civic Park School, with plans to hold it annually. The neighborhood celebrated its centennial in 2019 with various activities. The Civic Park Neighborhood Association organizes various activities, as well as neighborhood churches, such as Joy Tabernacle.

NORTH OF DOWNTOWN:
A TALE OF TWO ADJACENT REDEVELOPMENTS

In the 1950s, the neighborhoods north of downtown were a thriving area. But in the 1950s and 1960s, businesses closed, and residences moved. Homes then fell into disrepair. While the Doyle Urban Renewal project was already underway in the 1970s, by the 1980s, the city was continuing to buy homes and tear them down.

In 1980, to the immediate north of the Doyle urban renewal area north of downtown, North Saginaw Street still had a few thriving businesses. There were MacGregor Tire Company, Smith Loans (also Celebrity Car Company), Regal Furniture, Quality Glass, Austin's Paint & Floor Covering, the Belmont Hotel, R.A. Shaw & Company painting, Soul Beat Record Shop, Suggs Auto Service and Alford Auto Sales, along with a sizable apartment building. But as the neighborhood declined, the businesses disappeared one by one. MacGregor Tire closed by 1982. The Belmont Hotel, as well as Suggs Auto Service, closed in 1983. Austin's Paint and the Soul Beat Record Shop were gone by 1985.

By 1989, the only businesses remaining were Smith Financial Services/ Celebrity Car Company, Quality Glass, Newcomb Apartments, the Rice Bowl Restaurant and Alford Auto Sales. The remaining places were either closed or torn down. By 1991, the remaining businesses closed.

In 1996, Mayor Woodrow Stanley proposed Flint's new subdivision in more than thirty years. While there were doubts about the viability of the project, he noted that the River Village development in the Doyle Urban Renewal area was fully occupied. It took two years for plans to be drawn up and submitted.

In 1998, the Flint City Council approved plans for the sixty-eight-acre University Park Estates. The plan was to replace the conventional grid street pattern in the new subdivision bounded by North Saginaw Street to the west, Harriet Street to the north, Industrial Avenue to the east and Cornelia Street to the south with culs-de-sac. Constructed in two phases, portions of former streets were used as part of new culs-de-sac. In phase one, which the city council approved, part of Elizabeth Street became Columbia Drive, part of Wood Street became Loyola Drive, part of Mary Street became Spellman Drive and part of North Street became Loyola Drive.

The following year, thirty-six people reserved lots in University Park Estates. The refundable $2,000 deposit meant that more than half of the sixty-three lots in the subdivision's first phase were spoken for. In 2000, four model homes were built, and plans for the replat of the subdivision of phase one were submitted to the state. More than sixty homes priced between $100,000 and $160,000 were built in phase one. Buyers received significant tax breaks because the development was inside the city's Renaissance Zone approved by the state, which promoted development of struggling areas.

One complication in getting the development off the ground was a legal process called plat vacation, because the new subdivision discarded old lot designs from when century-old subdivision plat maps were originally drawn. That required a court hearing handled by the Michigan attorney general's office. Another complication was an environmental analysis, which the Michigan Department of Environmental Quality gave approvals for, allowing for construction.

By 2001, while additional houses were being built, families were moving in. But unlike suburban developments with shopping a short distance away, the closest major retail shopping areas were across town in either Flint Township or Burton. Funding issues delayed additional development of the subdivision in 2002.

In 2003, plans for phase two, with sixty more homes, were introduced, which added additional lots and streets to the project. For the additional cul-de-sac streets, part of Page Street became Wilberforce Drive. But an eighty-six-year-old homeowner holding out on the redrawing of property lines as well as a court hearing and friendly persuasions from the judge, the city and an attorney allowed her to agree to sign off on an agreement that led to phase two's development. The old house in question is still standing today on Cornelia Street. A $2 million grant from the C.S. Mott Foundation paved the way for construction of an additional forty-four homes.

With more than half of the phase two lots already sold, construction began in 2004 with houses priced in the $120,000 to $200,000 price range, with homeowners getting Renaissance Zone tax breaks.

West of North Saginaw Street, in 2001, another related urban renewal project was underway called Smith Village. Bounded by Mary Street to the north, North Saginaw Street to the east, Fifth Avenue to the south and Martin Luther King Avenue to the west, unlike University Park, the redevelopment would use existing streets and lots from the old plat maps. The southern part of Smith Village dates to the platting of the Village of Grand Traverse in 1837. The Smith Village Neighborhood Development District would oversee the construction of new homes, demolition of abandoned structures and renovation of existing homes worth saving. It would also make other improvements in the area west of University Park Estates.

Flint planned $6 million in federal grants to get Smith Village off the ground to build new homes and renovate old homes in the area with the funds from the Department of Housing and Urban Development (HUD). Both Smith Village and University Park made up the city's federal Homeownership Zone. Totaling 195 acres, it was supposed to produce three hundred new homes, with half for federally subsidized housing. In 2003, only a handful of homes in Smith Village were rehabilitated or built, and none of the new homes were occupied, which caught HUD's attention. There were concerns that HUD would ask Flint to give back $1.4 million allocated for Smith Village.

Unlike University Park, the Smith Village homes would be more affordably priced at less than $100,000. There were also disputes about whether Smith Village homes would include duplexes, with calls for only single-family homes. Only a few of the finished homes were occupied in 2004, but there were still too many vacant lots and trash-strewn abandoned homes. That year, the Michigan State Housing Development Authority provided funding to the Metro Housing Partnership (now known as Metro Community Development) to help first-time home buyers with down payments and up to $20,000 for needed home repairs. The repairs include fixing or replacing electrical, roofing, plumbing, heating, siding, foundation, insulation or windows. The rehab funds can be paired with a $5,000 down payment loan, which is forgiven if a homeowner lives there for five years.

But by 2008, only six new homes were built in Smith Village, and three of them were vacant. The problem in comparing Smith Village with University Park is that University Park was developed on already cleared land while Smith Village required the city to buy land and attempt to build a new neighborhood in the middle of a blighted area. The six built houses in 2008 were on Root Street in the middle of nowhere and were not attractive to potential buyers. One proposal to build additional houses in Smith Village in 2008 was to move planned houses from Stone Street in Carriage Town after a Chippewa burial ground containing the remains of sixty-seven people was uncovered where the eight houses were planned.

Fast-forward to 2011, and the proposed additional houses were never built. Genesee County at that time had a surplus of twenty-seven thousand vacant homes, so there was little incentive to build new homes with the glut of vacant housing in the area. At that time, housing values fell more than 30 percent since 2005, and nearly seven thousand properties slid into foreclosure. To avoid having to forfeit HUD money, twenty-seven modular

Vacant lots at Smith Village. *Gary Flinn.*

homes were completed at the end of the year. Twenty homes built from scratch were planned to be built in 2012.

In 2019, and even as this is written, there were still numerous vacant lots in Smith Village. Flint had to spend $81,000 to repair three vandalized vacant homes the city owned that year. The city also faced a March 31, 2019 deadline to sell the property or risk having to repay funds to the Michigan Stage Housing Development Authority. Houses in that area were advertised for sale in 2015, starting at $45,000.

Even though Smith Village was turning out to be a neighborhood boondoggle compared to University Park, there is hope for the future for the neighborhood, mentioned in the Hope for the Future section.

LOSS OF CONTROL

The loss of much of the city of Flint's tax base due to the job losses as employment opportunities left the area and put the city in an economic squeeze. After the recall of Mayor Woodrow Stanley on March 5, 2002, the city's $30 million budget hole was exposed. So, on May 22, Michigan governor John Engler declared a financial emergency in Flint. He appointed retiring Baker College CEO Ed Kurtz as Flint's emergency financial manager (EFM). City administrator Darnell Earley became acting mayor, serving until James Rutherford was elected in August to serve the remainder of Stanley's term.

The city waged a legal fight, spending more than $245,000, only to lose the court battle in October. Over the next two years, Kurtz issued 120 city directives, including closing recreation centers and the ombudsman's office, raising water bills by 11 percent, laying off city workers and approving sewer and road improvements of more than $1 million.

Businessman Don Williamson was elected mayor in November 2003 and butted heads with Kurtz. In June 2004, Kurtz recommended ending the state takeover.

In 2011, a new emergency manager law was enacted, giving EFMs additional authority, including altering collective bargaining agreements. Flint was again determined to be in "financial emergency," and Mayor Dayne Walling declined to request a hearing on the state's findings, and the city council voted not to appeal. Michael Brown was appointed EFM on November 29. He eliminated pay for the mayor and city council members, laid off several city officials and shut down the ombudsman's office and civil service commission.

In 2012, Michigan governor Rick Snyder reopened the Flint city lockup and boosted state police patrols of the city. Several city unions reached tentative agreements with EFM Brown, who adopted the 2013 budget and imposed concessions for two city unions. The budget included a $66 street light assessment and $143 trash collection fee replacing a waste collection tax.

Also in 2012, a petition drive to repeal the new EFM law was successful and placed on the ballot. That November, Michigan voters approved the law's repeal, forcing the departure of Brown. Kurtz returned as EFM under the old law. But the state legislature approved, and Snyder signed a replacement EFM law the following month.

The new replacement EFM law went into effect in March 2013. Kurtz was retained as EFM, but he resigned in July. Snyder appointed Brown again to be EFM, but Brown resigned in September, due to family concerns. Former Flint city administrator and acting mayor Earley returned as EFM after serving as Saginaw's city manager.

Darnell Earley was the EFM who oversaw the decision in April 2014 to change the city's water source from the Detroit water system to the reopened Flint Water Plant. This would treat Flint River water until a new water pipeline from Lake Huron to Flint, under construction by the Karegnondi Water Authority (KWA), was completed. While the city council approved switching the water source from Detroit to the KWA, it never approved using river water. The water plant was far from ready when Mayor Walling flipped the switch in the water plant, replacing Detroit water to treated river water, and the complaints started coming shortly afterward.

Snyder appointed Earley as Detroit Public Schools EFM on January 2015 and appointed Gerald Ambrose, who had served as the Flint EFM's financial advisor, as Flint's new EFM. While the city council voted in March 2015 to reconnect to the Detroit water system, Ambrose vetoed that move. On April 29, Ambrose left city hall, and a Receivership Transition Advisory Board (RTAB) took over managing city finances—but not before he signed orders that restricted Flint officials from revising any of his past actions for at least one year after receivership ended.

As the water complaints piled on, early warning signs were missed. The General Motors Flint Engine Plant was allowed to switch back to Detroit water because the river water was corroding machinery. That was because the water plant failed to add a corrosion control chemical to the river water, so water ate away at the protective coating that kept the lead in lead pipes from leaching into the water. That caused the excessive lead levels in drinking water that was causing permanent brain damage in Flint's small children, as Dr. Mona Hanna-Attisha determined. This finally convinced state and federal authorities that Flint's water was poisoning children. The regional Environmental Protection Agency office became toothless in 2008 after regional administrator Mary Gade was fired for raising the ire of politicians by forcing major employer Dow Chemical to speed up removal of toxic dioxin waste from Saginaw-area rivers. On October 16, 2015, Flint reconnected to the Detroit water system.

On April 4, 2018, Flint returned to local control.

THE FLINT WATER CRISIS AFTERMATH

On January 19, 2016, during Michigan's State of the State address, Governor Rick Snyder apologized to the people of Flint for the state's role

The author's parkway is dug up to reveal that the service line to the house was copper to begin with. The address on the white board is censored. *Gary Flinn.*

in causing the Flint Water Crisis and promised state funding to help affected residents and make infrastructure improvements. President Barack Obama signed an emergency declaration on January 16 providing federal help to the city.

The Michigan National Guard was activated to help distribute bottled water and faucet filters, which were first distributed at fire stations. Distribution was expanded the following August to water points of distribution, or PODs, located in each of Flint's nine wards, offering bottled water, bags to store empty bottles for recycling and filters. Governor Snyder discontinued the PODs in 2018, because he stated there were improvements in water quality from testing. The PODs were replaced by three help centers run by churches, which operate once a week on different days. As of this writing in early 2021, on the days they are open, there are still long lines of cars waiting for bottled water because of distrust by some Flint residents.

In 2016, Congress approved funding for the Flint Registry, led by Dr. Mona Hanna-Attisha. Open to anyone exposed to Flint water from April 2014 until October 2015, when the city was using river water, the registry allowed Flint residents affected by the water crisis, especially children, to be monitored regarding their development following lead poisoning.

The Flint Water Crisis brought national and international attention to the city. It also showed Flint to be the canary in a coal mine regarding lead service lines in other municipal water systems. In 2017, plumbing expert Richard Trethewey of the PBS TV series *This Old House* visited Flint to check out Mayor Karen Weaver's Fast Start program, and video was shot of the installation of a copper service line replacing the lead service line.

As was stated in my previous book *Hidden History of Flint*, my own water received regular testing, and the problem was found with my own plumbing, which is copper with mostly lead solder joints. The main problem was found with the kitchen faucet, which like many older faucets contained lead. On August 24, 2016, I received a free replacement kitchen faucet and under-sink filter. Even though my bathroom faucet is fine, a faucet filter is installed on it. My bathroom also has a shower head filter. Since the book was published, crews continued to inspect and replace lead service lines. As of this writing, the most recent water test was conducted by the newly formed McKenzie

Ditch Witch set up in front of the author's home, boring a hole leading to the neighbor's basement across the street and then used to pull the new copper service line to the water main. *Gary Flinn.*

Patrice Croom Flint Community Lab at the Flint Development Center inside the former Bunche Community School. The test result dated October 30, 2020, was 0.0839 parts per billion of lead, with the EPA Action Level being 15 parts per billion.

It should be noted that because of sloppy record keeping over the years, many homes had no record of the metal of their water service lines. Lead service lines were generally found in homes built before 1940. So, in August 2018, the front yard of my 1941 vintage house was dug up to inspect my water service line. As I had expected, because the pipe leading from my basement floor to the main shut off valve was made of copper, the service line at the city's shut off valve under my parkway was copper.

In June 2019, my neighbor's house, built in 1927, had the lead service line replaced. A Ditch Witch was set up in my front yard to bore a hole under the street to underneath the neighbor's basement. A square hole was cut on the neighbor's basement floor, which allowed the new copper service line to be attached to the boring pipe, and the Ditch Witch pulled the new service line to the water main.

Part III

HOPE FOR THE FUTURE

REDEVELOPING BUICK CITY

After what was left of Buick City closed in 2010, the remaining GM Powertrain factories were torn down, leaving a vast 452-acre land mass. After General Motors filed for Chapter 11 bankruptcy protection in 2009, a settlement was reached in 2011 that led to the formation of the Revitalizing Auto Communities Environmental Response (RACER) Trust, which took over ownership of former GM factory locations, including the Buick City site.

While brownfield cleanup of the site used for manufacturing for more than a century would take several years, finding new uses for portions of the land became ongoing.

The first major development took place in 2014, when construction on eighteen acres at the north end of the Buick City site was approved by the city on the American Spiral Weld Pipe factory, which manufactures pipelines. Completed the following December and employing at least fifty people, it makes sixty- and sixty-six-inch diameter pipes. This company made the pipeline used for the aforementioned KWA pipeline from Lake Huron to Genesee County, serving most of the out-county water customers.

On October 8, 2017, a portion of the south end of old Buick City at the corner of Hamilton Avenue and North Street saw new life when ground was broken for Lear Corporation's General Motors seating group plant. The

The Lear Corporation factory on Hamilton Avenue on part of the old Buick City site. *Gary Flinn.*

156,000-square-foot plant at 902 East Hamilton Avenue opened in April 2018, employing about six hundred workers.

In 2018, the C.S. Mott Foundation and the Michigan Economic Development Corporation announced a $23 million project to develop an environmentally friendly industrial park with at least 300,000 square feet of warehouse and light industrial space. Projected to bring three hundred permanent fulltime jobs, it would include walking and biking trails and possibly have an additional 700,000 square feet of light industrial space. But without commitments from companies to occupy the site in the southern portion of Buick City, a pass through of the site in the fall of 2020 showed no progress.

One hope for the future of the Buick City site came with the announcement in 2019 that it was in the running for a new factory that could bring up to two thousand jobs from Mahindra Automotive North America, which would build delivery vehicles for the U.S. Postal Service. But the COVID-19 pandemic delayed Mahindra's decision of which location among the four sites proposed, including Buick City, would get the factory.

Meanwhile in 2020, the Michigan Department of Environment, Great Lakes and Energy has taken over oversight of Buick City cleanup from the federal Environmental Protection Agency.

DOWNTOWN FLINT DEVELOPMENTS

Trying to boost downtown Flint following the move of commercial commerce to the suburbs ultimately led to a chicken and egg situation. After 5:00 p.m. on weekdays, downtown turned into a ghost town. So, a solution is to add residential housing downtown. First Street Lofts was developed in the former First National Bank building at the corner of Saginaw and First Streets in 2006. Two notable buildings opened with loft apartments, the Wade Trim Building in 2008 and the Rowe Professional Services Building in 2009. In 2010, the long-abandoned former Durant Hotel on Second Avenue between North Saginaw Street and M.L. King Avenue was converted into apartments. In 2014, the Flint Farmers Market moved downtown into the renovated former *Flint Journal* production and distribution center, boosting downtown activity considerably. Downtown Flint is also home to the University of Michigan–Flint. But it was considered a commuter college, and most students live in the immediate Flint area. In 2008, the university opened the First Street Residence Hall, the first on-campus residence hall for UM–Flint students. But that was just the beginning.

University of Michigan–Flint Campus Expansion Downtown

Expansion of the University of Michigan–Flint campus began with the acquisition of Northbank Center in 1998. It consists of the twelve-story former Industrial Savings Bank building, built in 1923, and the three-story former Consumers Power office building, also built in the 1920s. These are connected by a two-story building, built in 1986, designed to blend in with the others.

In 1990, the university acquired the closed Water Street Pavilion, which became University Pavilion after renovations. In 2002, the William S. White Building was constructed on the former site of the failed AutoWorld theme park north of the Flint River. All of these expansions extended the boundaries of the university's campus. But that was just the beginning. In 2015, the university's boundaries extended west of Saginaw Street with the purchase of the old Citizens Bank north tower, built in 1978, from FirstMerit Bank (since absorbed into Huntington Bank). Later in 2015, the university received one of the largest donations in its history. That was when on-campus housing expanded greatly with the addition of the Riverfront Residence Hall and Banquet Center, originally built as the Hyatt Regency.

Capitol Theatre Restoration

Easily the most beautiful building in downtown Flint is the Capitol Theatre building, built in 1927 and opened on January 19, 1928. Designed by world renowned architect John Eberson (1875–1955), it is one of the few remaining atmospheric theaters he designed that is still standing and in operation. The auditorium is designed to look like an outdoor Roman patio. Along with storefronts, it includes an arcade with offices upstairs on the second and third floors. In the basement was a recreation center, including a bowling alley. The theater was operated by W.S. Butterfield Theatres from the day it opened to when it first closed in 1976. It was sold the following year to local grocer George Farah. He and his family operated the theater on and off as a movie theater and concert venue. Former city councilman Woody Etherly, along with at least two others at different times, briefly operated the theater unsuccessfully. Troy Farah and Joel Rash staged concerts there in the 1990s, until the heating boiler broke down beyond repair in 1996. From the 1970s through the 1990s, notable performers who graced the Capitol's stage included AC/DC, April Wine, Black Sabbath, Ray Charles, the Go-Gos, John Mellencamp, Mitch Ryder, the Romantics and Mel Tillis. While the theater was dormant, it was kept in repair, and two regular gas furnaces were installed in front of the stage to keep the theater from freezing.

The Farah family also did partial restoration of the interior, and the Ruth Mott Foundation funded exterior repairs. Under private ownership, funds could not be raised for a full restoration. So, the theater was sold in 2015 to the Friends of the Capitol Theatre, which began a $37 million restoration the following year. The Charles Stewart Mott Foundation helped the project with a $15 million grant. The restoration project reversed a 1957 remodeling (or should that be "remuddling") and brought the theater back to pretty much its original 1928 appearance while meeting modern building codes. As part of the restoration, a later addition to the third story was removed to restore balance to the front façade. The refreshment stand was moved from the lobby to the arcade area. The removal of the non-original refreshment stand revealed the original paint colors under the balcony, which was preserved in the back of the theater marked off by a gold border. The basement includes additional handicap-accessible restrooms, a reception area and a green room, along with a small black box theater where intimate concerts could be staged.

The new Capitol Theatre attraction board is installed on the marquee. *Gary Flinn.*

Outside, the 1940s marquee design was duplicated on the new marquee using LED lighting, and the new duplicate vertical sign is lit with LED light bulbs. Lost and damaged terra-cotta was duplicated in the restoration. Whiting Auditorium management is running the restored theater, which can show movies with its Christie digital projector in the projection booth. Even though the Barton theater organ that was at the Capitol Theatre was moved to the Flint Institute of Music's MacArthur Recital Hall after the theater first closed, Whiting management believes that it would get more use where it is now, so there are no plans to install a vintage theater organ. The theater held its grand reopening with a free holiday show on December 8, 2017.

Dryden Building/The Ferris Wheel

In 1902, carriage maker William A. Patterson built the Dryden Building, named after his wife's family, at the southeast corner of South Saginaw and East Second Streets. Originally a six-story building, it was reduced to five stories when it was rebuilt following a fire in 1926. Along with offices upstairs,

The Dryden Building and the Ferris Wheel. *Gary Flinn.*

the main floor had storefronts, including a mezzanine. Over the years, J.C. Penney, Rosenthal's, Hills Bros., Flint Woolen Company, Heitzner's, Wendland's and a U.S. Post Office occupied the main floor.

By 2013, the Dryden Building had become dilapidated, with water damage in the basement and leftover equipment throughout the building. That year, Phil Hagerman, CEO of Diplomat Pharmacy and SkyPoint Ventures, bought it with plans to located SkyPoint Ventures on the fourth floor, the Hagerman Foundation on the fifth floor, office space and room for businesses on the second and third floors and space for several retailers in both the first floor and mezzanine.

In renovating the Dryden Building, the exterior was restored to its original appearance, and surviving historic details were restored. It opened in 2017, with both SkyPoint and the Hagerman Foundation occupying the fifth floor. The project spilled over into the adjacent Ferris Bros. Building.

In 2016, SkyPoint bought the seven-story building on South Saginaw next to the Dryden Building. Originally built in the 1920s to house Gainey

Furniture, it later became known as the home of Ferris Bros. Furs. A bookstore occupied the first floor before it sat empty for nearly thirty years.

With forty thousand square feet of space, it was renovated to serve as a business incubator to benefit entrepreneurs. Offering month-to-month rents, it gives businesses, professionals and freelancers a downtown presence and ways to give tenants ideas to bounce around to benefit everyone working there.

In a play on the most noted occupant in this building's history, it was given the whimsical name of the Ferris Wheel. One noted tenant that occupies the main floor in both the Dryden Building and the Ferris Wheel is the Foster Coffee Company.

The Marketplace

When the YWCA vacated its high-rise building for the more manageable Phoenix Building, the old YWCA was torn down in 2018 to make way for a new residential development called the Marketplace. Developed by

The Marketplace apartment building, where the YWCA used to stand. *Gary Flinn.*

Uptown Reinvestment Corp with help from the Michigan State Housing Development Authority, they began planning for its development in 2016.

It was designed by the Lansing-based firm of Studio Intrigue Architects. Flint-based DW Lurvey Construction was the general contractor.

Construction began on the $19.5 million complex consisting of ninety-two units at the start of 2018 and was completed at the end of the year. It's a mixed-income residence, with rent ranging from $500 to $1,200 per month, based on size and the renter's income. Four stories high, it has seventy-five apartments, seventeen townhouses and 4,600 square feet of commercial space in four retail units. The apartments range between 675 and 950 square feet, while the adjacent two-story townhouses range from 1,000 to 1,200 square feet.

Amenities there include a fitness center, a community center, a gazebo, a barbecue area and a playground. Located a block away from the Flint Farmers Market, it was developed to cater to families and provide additional housing downtown.

Mott Community College Culinary Institute

One notable vacant downtown building was the former F.W. Woolworth store at the northwest corner of South Saginaw and Second Streets. Built in 1920 and remodeled inside and out in the 1950s, the store closed in 1970, when it moved to the new Genesee Valley Center in Flint Township. Eventually, a fast-food restaurant took over part of the space, which it renovated inside and out, and a plasma center, along with a jewelry store, gift shop and dollar store also operated in the building at one time or another.

The entire building was vacant for several years, until 2017, when Mott Community College announced plans to establish a culinary school there. Exterior renovations from the 1950s and 1970s were removed to reveal the original façade, which was restored. Inside, the thirty-six-thousand-square-foot building includes state-of-the-art culinary kitchens, baking and pastry kitchens, a meat fabrication laboratory, a confections laboratory and a specially ventilated cool area for preparing cold dishes.

Instead of a Woolworth-style lunch counter, fine dining is offered at the Applewood Café, which is open for lunch while classes are in session. The Coffee Beanery also has a location inside.

The Mott Community College Culinary Institute in the former Woolworth's store. *Gary Flinn.*

Hilton Garden Inn

In 1920, the Genesee County Savings Bank moved into its new eleven-story bank building at 352 South Saginaw Street at Kearsley Street. In 1928, the five-story Sherman Building was built behind the bank building at 110 West Kearsley Street and Buckham Alley. One notable aspect of that building is that the upper four floors are cantilevered over Buckham Alley.

In 1947, the Italian Renaissance Revival–style bank building was remodeled to add Art Deco details. At the same time, the Sherman Building was connected to the bank building on each floor. When Genesee County Savings Bank merged with the Merchants & Mechanics Bank in 1957, the combined bank became Genesee Merchants Bank & Trust Company, headquartered in this bank building. It continued to serve as Genesee Bank's headquarters, to give the short marketing name, until 1968, when it moved to Genesee Towers. The old headquarters then became a bank branch for a few years. The Genesee Merchants Bank neon signs at both ends of the

The former Genesee County Savings Bank Building is now the Hilton Garden Inn. *Gary Flinn.*

The entrance
to the Hilton
Garden Inn.
Gary Flinn.

bank building remained until the bank was absorbed into NBD Bank, N.A. (since absorbed into Chase) in 1990.

The former bank building changed hands a few times. Odyssey Housing Development owned it until 2000, when Citizens Bank bought it to house offices. Citizens sold it in 2003 to Daystar Development. Over time, the number of tenants decreased, until it became empty when the U.S. Department of Housing and Urban Development moved out.

After sitting vacant for twenty years and becoming a magnet for vandals and graffiti, including when someone in 2009 hung a protest banner from the roof, it was announced in 2018 that both the old Genesee Bank building and the adjacent Sherman Building would be redeveloped as a Hilton Garden Inn. That year, two vacant buildings on West Kearsley, between

Beach Street and Buckham Alley, were torn down to make way for Buckham Square behind the hotel, which is a flexible public green space that can house food trucks.

The $36.5 million project received financing from the nonprofit Uptown Reinvestment Corp, which owns the building, along with the Michigan Economic Development Corp, the C.S. Mott Foundation, Skypoint Ventures and Local Initiatives Support Corp, along with Huntington Bank and Old National Bank. Crescent Hotels & Resorts is managing the 101-room hotel, which includes a full-service restaurant in the main lobby, a meeting and banquet center and a rooftop lounge atop the Sherman Building, which houses twenty-one of the hotel's rooms. It officially opened on November 2, 2020.

The restaurant is Sauce Italian American Kitchen. The old bank vault was made into a private dining area. The Federal Coffee House is also open during the day, and the Simmer Rooftop Lounge is open seasonally. The hotel has a staff of forty-five full-time and fifteen part-time employees.

Recalling what happened with the Hyatt Regency and its later incarnations to its present use by UM–Flint as a residence hall, maybe with the new developments that occurred following the start of the water crisis, this hotel can be successful. Kraemer Design Group, which developed the old Durant Hotel, was the architect of this project, which restores the bank building's historic details.

Downtown Bars and Restaurants

Along with long-established hangout spots, such as the Torch Lounge on Buckham Alley, established in 1966; the White Horse Tavern on West Court Street, opened in 1973; and Churchill's on South Saginaw Street, founded in 1980, the addition of the University of Michigan–Flint downtown campus and new downtown housing allowed for the establishment of additional downtown hangout spots, which restored an active night life to downtown Flint. They include occupants of the Flint Farmers Market, which was relocated downtown in 2014. The following are additional places that opened:

The Loft, 515 Buckham Alley, 2003
Soggy Bottom Bar, 613 Martin Luther King Ave., 2003
Hoffman's Deli, 444 South Saginaw St., 2008
Blackstone's, 531 South Saginaw St., 2009

Blackstone's Smokehouse restaurant and Wade Trim building. *Gary Flinn.*

Flint Crepe Company, 555 South Saginaw St., 2009
Raspberries Rhythm Cafe & Bar, 448 South Saginaw St., 2009
Cork on Saginaw, 635 South Saginaw St., 2011
501 Bar & Grill, 500 South Saginaw St., 2013
Cafe Rhema, 432 South Saginaw St., 2013
Soriano's Mexican Kitchen, 836 South Saginaw St., 2017
The Eberson, 130 East Second St., 2019
Xolo, 555 South Saginaw St., 2019

IMPROVEMENTS TO BERSTON FIELD HOUSE

When the history of the nearly century-old Berston Field House was described in my previous book *Hidden History of Flint*, published in 2017, the landmark at the corner of North Saginaw Street and Pasadena Avenue on Flint's North Side was very active with plans for the future. That year,

Top: Berston Field House in 1923. *Courtesy of Bryant Nolden.*

Bottom: The long-gone Berston Field House pool *Courtesy of Bryant Nolden.*

it received funding from the C.S. Mott Foundation to assess the building's physical needs. Even though the facility's two basketball courts saw use by several future basketball stars, they are not of regulation size.

Ongoing programs that Berston hosts are the Creative Expression Dance Studio, boxing, the Chosen Few Arts Council, the Berston Bicycle Club Project, Enhance Fitness, YMCA Safe Places, the Senior Line Dance Smooth Steppers, the Berston Inner City Softball League, basketball, 100K Ideas (offering entrepreneurial help), Success Happens (offering help in training and improving academic performance), a weight room and yoga.

Thanks to the Arts Education and Cultural Enrichment Millage, which Genesee County voters approved in 2018, Berston Field House has funding for its ongoing programs for a decade. The assessment for the facility's needs led to plans to expand and renovate Berston Field House in a $14 million expansion. In February 2020, Berston Field House executive director Bryant Nolden signed a twenty-five-year lease with the City of Flint, which owns the facility, paving the way for the historic landmark's expansion.

While the front façade facing Saginaw Street will remain unchanged, the improvements will take place in the back. With hopes of purchasing the former Parkland School site from the Mount Hermon Baptist Church to expand the field behind Berston, a new modern gymnasium will be added to the back of Berston, offering more versatility and seating 150 spectators. It will be made available to Amateur Athletic Union teams, as well as other organized basketball games. The new expanded Berston Field House is expected to open in 2023.

COMMUNITIES FIRST OFFERS QUALITY AFFORDABLE HOUSING

In 2010, the nonprofit Communities First was founded by Flint natives Glenn and Essence Wilson to boost economic development by offering affordable housing and innovative programming to build healthy and vibrant communities. Their first project was in 2014, when they renovated the 1908 vintage Oak School into a twenty-four-unit low-income senior housing facility, which opened in September 2015.

Their next project began in 2015—renovating the long-abandoned Swayze Apartments, built in 1924 by Buick cofounder William Ballenger Sr. at the corner of West Court Street and Grand Traverse. The $8.3 million project included not just renovating the apartment building also building an additional similar apartment building next door, with a total of thirty-six apartment units in the two buildings. It was completed in December 2016 and opened with a ribbon-cutting ceremony, with Bill Ballenger, grandson of the builder, attending on March 31, 2017.

In 2015, Flint Community Schools approved the sale of the closed and vandalized Coolidge School on Flint's west side, on Van Buren Avenue near Ballenger Highway and Beecher Road. Built in 1929 with additional

The Coolidge Park Apartments dedication in the former Coolidge Community School, with mayor Sheldon Neeley cutting the ribbon with small scissors and the author seen above the white balloon wearing a cap. *Ivonne Raniszewski.*

Georgia Manor Apartments on Lyon Street before renovation began. *Gary Flinn.*

classrooms built in 1951 and a gymnasium built in 1970, it had been closed for four years. Construction began in 2018. Along with renovating the school into apartments and a community center, an additional four-story apartment building with ground-floor storefronts was built along Ballenger Highway. On its completion in September 2019, I was invited as a part of the Coolidge community to take part in its dedication. It was a matter of personal pride because of my concern about that school's future.

New construction on Ballenger Highway north of Flushing Road began in 2019 with the three-story Berkley Place Apartments, with thirty-three units of one- and two-bedroom apartments. The land was acquired from the Genesee County Land Bank in 2017 and is within walking distance of a grocery store, a pharmacy, medical services, a barber and a bus stop. It opened in December 2020.

Communities First bought the abandoned three-story Georgia Manor Apartments, built in 1966 at the corner of Lyon Street and First Avenue, and began renovating them in October 2020, offering twenty units for families with a range of incomes and providing a boost to the Carriage Town neighborhood.

Communities First works with several partners, including the Ruth Mott Foundation, Michigan Local Initiatives Support Corp., Charles Stewart

Mott Foundation, Hagerman Foundation, A.G. Bishop Charitable Trust, Nartel Family Foundation, City of Flint, Corporation for Supportive Housing, Community Foundation of Greater Flint, BEST Project, Genesee County Land Bank Authority, Michigan State Housing Development Authority, U.S. Department of Housing and Urban Development, TCF Bank, PNC Bank, Chase Bank, Huntington Bank and Michigan Community Resources .

CLARK COMMONS BREATHING NEW LIFE TO SMITH VILLAGE

There were two problems the city of Flint had to face in recent years. One was the failure of the Atherton East public housing development built in 1967 on an isolated floodplain of Flint's southeast side that had become a flood-prone crime haven. The other was the development of Smith Village north of downtown—or the lack of it due to the large number of vacant lots.

Atherton East was developed by the city to relocate residents displaced by expressway construction and the St. John urban renewal project. But it was isolated from the rest of the city by Thread Creek to the north, the Lake State Railway tracks to the west and the city of Burton to the east and south.

In 2018, Flint received a HUD Choice Neighborhoods Grant of $30 million from the Department of Housing and Urban Development to relocate residents of Atherton East to locations with better access to basic services and job opportunities. It was added onto a $1.5 million tax credit from the Michigan State Housing Development Authority. Among the locations chosen for many of the residents to move to was the newly announced plans for Clark Commons, which is being built in phases on vacant land at the aforementioned Smith Village development.

With the project developing in four phases, the first phase was built in 2019 and 2020, with sixty-two mixed income housing units, including thirty-nine new units for Atherton East residents. The second and third phases, to be built between 2021 and 2024, will also be in Smith Village. Phase four is also planned for 2021 and 2024 and will be in the Windiate Park area on Flint's south side on Pengelly Road off South Saginaw Street, alongside the planned Grand Traverse Greenway bicycle trail on the old CSX railroad right of way. It will connect with the recently developed Genesee Valley Trail on the old Grand Trunk right of way and the long-established Flint River Trail as part of the statewide Iron Belle Trail.

After all of the Atherton East residents are relocated, the buildings will be torn down and left as green space on the one-hundred-year floodplain.

APPENDIX

LOST SCHOOLS

High Schools

Central Community High School (1923–2009)
601 Crapo Street
Status: Vacant and deteriorating

(Old) Northern Community High School (1928–88)
401 East McClellan Street
Converted to Emerson Junior High School in 1971; converted to Flint
  Academy in 1976; merged with Southwestern High to form Flint
  Southwestern Academy in 1988; demolished in 1989

(New) Northern Community High School (1971–2013)
G-3284 Mackin Road
Status: Vacant and deteriorating

Northwestern Community High School (1964–2018)
G-2138 Carpenter Road
Converted to Flint Junior High in 2019; closed 2020
Status: Houses food services central kitchen

The closed Flint Central Community High School as it looked in 2020. *Gary Flinn.*

Schools of Choice (1927–2010)
517 East Fifth Avenue
Built as St. Michael Catholic School; leased to Flint Schools in 1973
Status: Original 1927 building razed in 2017; 1953 addition now Catholic
    Charities Center for Hope

Junior High Schools

Bryant Junior High (1958–2013)
201 East Pierson Road
Closed as junior high in 1988; converted to Mott Adult High School Bryant
    Center; converted to elementary school in 2002
Status: Vacant

Emerson Junior High (1925–1988)

316 East Pasadena Avenue

Operated as Emerson Intermediate from 1971 to 1976; converted to Flint Open School from 1976 to 1983; became Emerson Center in 1983; demolished in 1989

Longfellow Junior High (1928–2006)

1255 North Chevrolet Avenue

Status: Vacant and deteriorating

Lowell Junior High (1929–2003)

3301 North Vernon Avenue

Closed as junior high in 1988; private Valley School from 1990 to 1997; operated as Lowell Accelerated Academics Academy

Status: Vacant and deteriorating

McKinley Junior High (1930–2012)

4501 Camden Avenue

Status: Vacant and deteriorating

Lowell Junior High School after the aluminum windows and copper trim were stolen. *Gary Flinn.*

Whittier Junior High (1925–2008)
701 Crapo Street
Status: Vacant and deteriorating

Zimmerman Junior High (1924–2013)
2421 Corunna Road
Closed as junior high in 1994; became Mott Adult High School's Zimmerman Center
Status: Vacant and deteriorating

Elementary Schools

Anderson Community School (1965–2009)
G-3248 Mackin Road
Status: Sold to Empowerment Enterprise Inc.

Bunche Community School (1967–2012)
4121 M.L. King Avenue
Status: Now the Flint Development Center

Carpenter Road Community School (1965–2015)
6901 Webster Road
Status: Vacant and deteriorating

Civic Park Community School (1922–2009)
1402 West Dayton Street
Status: Vacant and deteriorating

Clark Community School (1912–1971)
1519 Harrison Street
Demolished in 2014

Cody Community School (1925–2003)
3029 Fenton Road
Demolished in 2012

Cook Community School (1917–2002)
500 Welch Boulevard
Status: Vacant and deteriorating

Coolidge Community School (1929–2011)
3615 Van Buren Avenue
Status: Now Coolidge Park Apartments

Cummings Community School (1956–2015)
G-2200 Walton Boulevard
First closed in 2008 and reopened in 2011
Status: Now Great Expectations Early Childhood Center

Dewey Community School (1921–91)
4419 North Saginaw Street
Status: Now Sylvester Broome Empowerment Village

Dort Community School, including **Flint Technical High School** (1911–2013)
601 Witherbee Street (2025 North Saginaw Street before 1963)
Second school built in 1917 (served as Flint Technical High School from 1939 to 1959); addition connecting both buildings built in 1963; 1911 and 1917 buildings razed and replaced in 1976
Status: Vacant and deteriorating

The original Dort School. *Author's collection.*

Fairview Community School (1915–1971)

1300 Leith Street

Later served as a drug abuse agency, Alternative Junior High School and then Flint Schools of Choice

Demolished 1976

Garfield Community School (1929–2009)

301 E. McClellan Street

Status: Vacant and deteriorating

Gundry Community School (1955–2008)

6031 Dupont Street

Status: Now Cathedral of Faith Ministries

Homedale Community School (1913–2003)

1501 Davison Road

Destroyed by fire in 2010

Jefferson Community School (1926–1988)

5306 North Street

Status: Now Second Chance Church of Flint

Johnson Community School (1967–2008)

5323 Western Rd.

Reopened as Johnson Accelerated Academics Academy after Lowell Junior High closed in 2002

Status: Vacant and deteriorating

Kennedy Community School (1940–1977)

1541 North Saginaw Street

Built as St. Paul Lutheran School; sold to Flint Schools in 1963 and named Mary Street School; renamed John F. Kennedy School in 1966

Demolished 2011

King Community School (1970–2006)

520 West Rankin Street

Early Childhood Center opened in 2006

Status: Vacant

Lawndale Avenue Community School (1951–2003)
3202 Forest Hill Avenue
Built as St. Luke Catholic School; leased to Flint Schools in 1995
Status: Now St. Luke's N.E.W. Life Center

Lewis Community School (1917–87)
3218 North Franklin Avenue
Converted to Lowell Junior High annex in 1969; became Lewis Center as
    Mott Adult High School in 1982
Demolished 1988

Lincoln Community School (1918–1988)
2820 South Saginaw Street
Status: Now International Academy of Flint

Manley Community School (1969–2003)
3002 Farley Street
Status: Vacant

Martin Community School (1924–2002)
6502 Stafford Place
Demolished in 2011

Merrill Community School (1953–2009)
1501 West Moore Street
Status: Vacant and deteriorating

Oak Community School (1908–1976)
1000 Oak Street
Status: Now Oak Street Senior Apartments

Parkland Community School (1913–76)
3319 North Street
Status: Most of school demolished in 1997; later addition vacant and
    deteriorating

Pierson Community School (1928–2002)
300 East Mott Avenue
Demolished in 2013

Scott Community School (1960–2016)
1602 South Averill Avenue
Status: Now Accelerated Learning Academy

Selby Community School (1956–1988)
5005 Cloverlawn Drive
Status: Now Eagles Nest Academy

Sobey Community School (1962–2003)
3701 North Averill Avenue
Status: Now Boys and Girls Club of Greater Flint

Summerfield Community School (1970–2012)
1360 Milbourne Avenue
Status: Now a preschool

Stevenson Community School (1909–82)
510 West Sixth Avenue
Demolished in 1982

Stewart Community School (1955–2009)
1950 Burr Boulevard
Status: Vacant and deteriorating

Walker Community School (1960–88)
817 East Kearsley Street
Status: Now Walker Center office building

Washington Community School (1922–2013)
1400 North Vernon Avenue
Status: Vacant and deteriorating

Wilkins Community School (1972–2010)
121 East York Avenue
Status: Vacant and deteriorating

Williams Community School (1969–2010)
3501 Minnesota Avenue
Status: Vacant and deteriorating

ADDITIONAL LOST BARS AND RESTAURANTS

Along with the lost bars and restaurants mentioned in the text, popular demand by followers of my books' Facebook page led to the listing of additional lost bars and restaurants in the city of Flint.

Downtown

Steadman's Cafeteria, West Kearsley Street
Uncle Bob's Diner, Harrison Street
Elias Brothers Big Boy, Harrison Street
Cromer's Restaurant, North Saginaw Street
A&W Drive-in, Beach Street near West Court Street
The Copa, South Saginaw Street
The Metropolis, South Saginaw Street
College Inn Hotel, Detroit Street (now MLK)
The Verdict, South Saginaw and Court Streets
The Press Room, East Second Street
Ken's Coney Island, South Saginaw Street
Sport's Bar & Sandwich Shop, Brush Alley
Yum-Yum Shoppe, East First Street
The Purple Cow, inside the Durant Hotel
Tom Z's, West Court Street
The Rose Bowl, in the Capitol Theatre Building

North Side

O'Toole's, North Saginaw Street and Flint Park Boulevard
Papa Joe's, North Saginaw Street
The Colonel's, North Saginaw Street
Casablanca Bar, Industrial Avenue
Jack Gilbert's Wayside Inn, Pasadena Avenue
Fireside Lounge, Pierson Road
The Country Squire, Pierson Road
Walli's, North Saginaw and Pierson Road
Squire Jack's Fish & Chips, Fleming Road
Ken Jo's, Detroit Street (now MLK)

Fifty Grand Cocktail Lounge, East Stewart Avenue
The Wagon Wheel, Richfield Road
Fifth Avenue Grill, Detroit Street (now MLK)
Edelhoff's, Dupont Street
The Beer Vault, Industrial Avenue
Town Talk Bar, North Saginaw Street
A&W, North Saginaw Street

South Side

Sunrise, Fenton Road
Varsity Car-Feteria, Fenton Road
Walli's, Center Road
Tip-Top Hamburger Shop, South Saginaw Street
Eighth Street Café, East Eighth Street
Bob & Ethel's Rib Crib, Lippincott Boulevard
Ad Lib Lounge, Grand Traverse
Sicily's Pizza, South Saginaw Street
Remington's, Fenton Road
Ron's Pizza & Ice Cream, Fenton Road
Al's, South Saginaw Street
Diamond Bar, South Saginaw Street
Payne's, South Saginaw Street
The Ice House, South Saginaw Street
Golden Steer, South Saginaw Street
The Happy Hour, Chevrolet Avenue
Zora's, Fenton Road

East Side

The Ivanhoe, Davison and Center Roads
The Red Rooster, Davison Road and Averill Avenue
John's Restaurant, Davison Road
Angelo's Coney Island, Davison Road and Franklin Avenue
Kenny's Place, Franklin Avenue
Broadway Coney Island, Franklin Avenue
Silver's Bar, Franklin Avenue

Howard Johnson's Motor Lodge and Restaurant on Center Road. *Author's collection.*

Mexican Village Café, Lewis Street
The Raincheck Lounge, Averill Avenue
Dawn Donuts, Davison Road
The Lamplighter Lounge, Longway Boulevard
Howard Johnson's, Center Road
Esquire Inn (also known as Elbow Inn), Western Road

West Side

Third Avenue Fish & Chips, West Third (now University) Avenue
Paddy McGee's, Flushing Road east of Ballenger Highway
Colonial Restaurant, Corunna Road
Higgins, Corunna Road
Laffety's Lounge, Asylum Street
Andy's Restaurant, Flushing Road
Gregory's, Ballenger Highway near Flushing Road
King's Armor, Ballenger and Flushing Roads
Wimpy's, Chevrolet Avenue
Ruggero's Pizzeria, Chevrolet Avenue

The long-gone Third Avenue Fish & Chips on Third (now University) Avenue. *Courtesy of Sharon Wilson.*

Sugar & Spice, Welch Boulevard
Lee's Famous Recipe, Corunna Road
Atlas Coney Island, Corunna Road

BIBLIOGRAPHY

Microfilm Reels

Flint Journal (*Flint Daily Journal* and *Flint Sunday Journal*), 1903–present.
Flint News-Advertiser, 1943–57.

Books and Periodicals

Bent, Don. *A Place Called Buick: A History of the GM Powertrain Flint North Site "The Buick," 1905–2005, Celebrating 100 Years of Automotive Manufacturing Excellence.* Flint, MI: Self-published, 2005.
———. *The History of GM Powertrain Flint North.* Fenton, MI: Rockman & Sons Publishing, 2005.
Bloomberg News. "A G.M. Unit Is Renamed." February 14, 1995.
Briggs, Lisa. "Berston Field House—Prepared for Growth." *My City,* May 2019.
Brooky, Kyle. *Abandoned Flint.* Stroud, UK: Fonthill Media, 2020.
Burr, C.B. "Oak Grove—A Memory." *Medical History of Michigan* 2 (1930): 759–61.
Chronology of the Industrial Mutual Association and Parent Organizations 1901–1963. Flint: Flint Public Library, 2013. [Copied from material in the library of the *Flint Journal.*]
City of Flint. *Civic Park Home Preservation Manual.* July 1981.

Committee of Sponsors for the Flint College and Cultural Development and the Flint Board of Education. *Flint's Community College and Cultural Center.* Flint, MI: N.p., 1958.

Corporate Remediation Group. *Site Remedial Action Plant Addendum, Former DuPont Flint Automotive Products Facility, Flint, Michigan.* Wilmington, DE: Corporate Remediation Group, April 2008.

Crawford, Kim. *The Daring Trader.* East Lansing: Michigan State University Press, 2012.

"Diocese of Lansing 1937–1962." *Catholic Weekly* 8, no. 44 (May 19, 1962).

Dybis, Karen. *Better Made in Michigan.* Charleston, SC: The History Press, 2015.

Evanoff, Michael W. *Through the Melting Pot and Beyond: The St. John Street Experience Flint's International Village: A Remembrance.* Midland, MI: Pendell Publishing, 1979.

Faires, Nora, and Nancy Hanflik. *Jewish Life in the Industrial Promised Land 1855–2005.* East Lansing: Michigan State University Press, 2005.

Faith 15, no. 5 (June 2015). Special edition.

Fine, Sidney. *The General Motors Strike of 1936–1937.* Ann Arbor: University of Michigan Press, 1969.

Flinn, Gary. "Christmas Past in Flint." *Your Magazine* 5, 12 (December 2008): 32–33.

———. "Flint Faience & Tile Company—GM's Artistic Side." *Your Magazine* 5, no. 4 (April 2008): 36–37.

———. "Flint's Dueling Amusement Parks." *Your Magazine* 6, no. 6 (June 2009): 36–37.

———. "A Long-Standing High School Tradition: Central vs. Northern Football." *Your Magazine* 5, no. 11 (November 2008): 36–37.

Flint Osteopathic Hospital, 1960. Dedication booklet.

"Flint Varnish Works Increases Capital." *Paint, Oil and Drug Review* 56, no. 23 (December 3, 1913): 38.

Gaiski, Stephen N. *Making It Right: Why Your Car Payments Are Lasting Longer Than Your Factory Paint Job.* Novi, MI: Zestar Corporation, 2009.

Genesee County Historical Society. *Flint, 1890–1960.* Charleston, SC: Arcadia Publishing, 2004.

———. *Picture Palaces & Movie Houses.* Flint, MI: Advertisers Press, 1999.

Gill, David. "Nicholas McKay, Lint Roller Inventor, Dies." *HFN*, November 25, 2014.

Gordon, Joanne. "Brushing Off Mom." *Forbes*, February 3, 2003.

"Greater Future for Flint Varnish." *Michigan Manufacturer and Financial Record* 21, no. 24 (June 15, 1918): 2.

Gustin, Lawrence R. *Picture History of Flint.* Grand Rapids, MI: William B. Eerdmans Publishing, 1976.

Hamady, Robert Lee. *Groceryman.* Pennsauken, NJ: Planigale Press, 2006.

Hauser, H.L., ed. "Oak Grove." *Headlight Flashes Along the Grand Trunk Railway System* 2, no. 12 (August 1896).

Highsmith, Andrew R. *Demolition Means Progress.* Chicago: University of Chicago Press, 2015.

Hillstrom, Kevin, and Laurie Collier Hillstrom, ed. *The Industrial Revolution in America.* Santa Barbara, CA: ABC-CLIO, 2006.

Hinterman, Peter. "Flint Through the Decades." *My City,* July, August, September, October and November 2019.

ICF International. *Civic Park Historic Residential District Report Summary.* 2013. http://www.thelandbank.org/downloads/3cp_hist_res_dist_rpt_summary.pdf

Industrial Mutual Association. *The I.M.A. News: Auditorium Souvenir Number,* September 12, 1929.

Lin, Jeremy C.F., and Haeyoun Park. "High Lead Levels Were Detected in Nearly 400 Flint Homes, and There May Be More. *New York Times,* February 6, 2016.

Mabbitt, Bob. "Delphi Abandons Confidential Employee Medical Records at Flint Plant." *Uncommon Sense,* February 2005.

———. "Delphi's Junk Status." *Uncommon Sense,* January 2005.

Manns, Myron. "Spencer's House Revisited. *MyCity,* December 2013.

McClelland, Edward. *Nothin' but Blue Skies.* New York: Bloomsbury Press, 2013.

Michigan Bell Telephone Company. *Flint Area Telephone Directory.* May 1971.

———. *Flint Area Telephone Directory.* May 1975.

Moser, Whet. "What Did the EPA Do Wrong in Flint?" *Chicago Magazine,* January 25, 2016. https://www.chicagomag.com.

"Oak Grove and Dr. Burr." *Journal Michigan State Medical Society.* Editorial reprint (September 1919).

Oak Grove Hospital. *Oak Grove: A Hospital for the Treatment of Nervous and Mental Diseases, Flint, Michigan.* Flint, MI: Oak Grove Hospital, 1896.

The Origin, Development, and Accomplishments of the Industrial Mutual Association and the Annual Report of the Industrial Mutual Association, Flint, Michigan July 1, 1936–June 30, 1937. Flint: Flint Public Library, 2013.

Pielack, Leslie K. *The Saginaw Trail.* Charleston, SC: The History Press, 2018.

Pound, Arthur. *The Turning Wheel.* Garden City, NY: Doubleday, Doran & Company, 1934.

Rhoads, Roxanne, and Joe Schipani. *Haunted Flint.* Charleston, SC: The History Press, 2019.

Rubenstein, James M. *The Changing US Auto Industry.* New York: Routledge, 1992.

Sherefkin, Robert, and David Sedgwick. "Gulda Ousted as CEO as Peregrine Falls Short." *Crain's Detroit Business,* February 2, 1998.

Sherefkin, Robert. "Peregrine May Shut Flint Plant." *Crain's Detroit Business,* March 23, 1998.

U.S. Senate Subcommittee on Labor. *General Motors Plant Closings.* Washington, D.C.: U.S. Government Printing Office, 1987.

Warnshuis, Fredrick W., ed. "State News Notes." *Journal of the Michigan State Medical Society* 19 (June 1920): 259–60.

Wood, Edwin O. *History of Genesee County Michigan: Her People, Industries and Institutions.* Indianapolis, IN: Federal Publishing, 1916.

Worth-Nelson, Jan. "Longtime Community Landmark Woodside Church Up for Sale." *East Village Magazine* 54, no. 12 (December 2016): 10–11.

Young, Gordon. *Teardown.* Berkeley: University of California Press, 2013.

Young, Katherine, and Joe Grimm. *Coney Detroit.* Detroit, MI: Wayne State University Press, 2012.

Brochures

Inland Fisher Guide Division, General Motors Corporation, Communications & Public Affairs. *At a Glance.* Warren, MI: Self-published, undated.

Internet Articles

Adamo Group. "Delphi Corporation—Delphi Flint West Complex". http://www.adamogroup.com/wp-content/uploads/2014/05/delphi-flint-west.pdf

———. "Delphi Flint East Case Study." https://www.adamogroup.com.

Carah, Jake. "New Housing Development Coming to Flint—Could Be the First of Three." FlintSide. November 20, 2017. https://www.flintside.com.

Carey, Darlene C. "Crowd 'Overjoyed' Downtown as MCC Culinary Arts Institute Opens." *East Village Magazine,* June 9, 2019. https://www.eastvillagemagazine.org.

Charles Stewart Mott Foundation. "Staging a Comeback." July 20, 2016. https://www.mott.org.

Darden, Joseph, Linda Jones and Julianne Price. "Ethnographic Evaluation of the Behavioral Causes of Undercount in a Black Ghetto of Flint, Michigan." U.S. Census Bureau. https://www.census.gov.

Davis, Ennis. "Adaptive Reuse: Flint's Water Street Pavilion." https://www.moderncities.com.

Environmental Protection Agency. "Hazardous Waste Cleanup: Buick City Facility—Flint, Michigan." https://www.epa.gov.

Flint Housing Commission. "South Flint Community Plan." July 2016. http://www.flinthud.org.

FlintSide. "Before and After: $8.3 Million Investment Transforms Historic Flint Building." April 3, 2017. https://www.flintside.com.

Florida, Richard. "Vacancy: America's Other Housing Crisis." *CityLab*, July 27, 2018. https://www.citylab.com.

Ford, Harold C. "Village Life: Encountering a "Child of God" in Resurgent Civic Park." *East Village Magazine*, March 1, 2018. https://www.eastvillagemagazine.org.

General Motors. "GM Powertrain—Past, Present, Future." 2008. https://web.archive.org.

Hayes, Patrick. "Vacant Carriage Town Apartment Complex to Get New Life." FlintSide, October 27, 2020. https://www.flintside.com.

Henderson, Tom. "Opinion: Flint's Politicians Deserve Blame for Water Problem." *Crain's Detroit Business*, January 24, 2016. https://www.crainsdetroit.com.

Imagine Flint. "Choice Neighborhood Initiative." https://www.imagineflint.com.

Jackson, David D. The American Automobile Industry in World War Two. https://usautoindustryworldwartwo.com.

Lawson, Ronald, and Eric Schenker. "Land and Property Values in Relation to Dort Highway Improvements." July 1960. https://www.michigan.gov.

Michigan Bids. "Adamo Demolition Company." https://www.michiganbids.us.

Michigan Department of State Police. "Report on Secure Cities partnership (SCP)." December 2017. https://www.michigan.gov.

Michigan Department of Technology, Management and Budget. "Demographic and Labor Market Profile: City of Flint." April 2016. https://milmi.org.

Michigan PFAS Action Team. "Coldwater Road Landfill, Flint, Genesee County." https://www.michigan.gov.

Michigan Railroad History. "Station: Flint, MI." http://www.michiganrailroads. com.

Nagl, Kurt. "$19.5 Million Mixed-Use Development Gets $7 Million from State." *Crain's Detroit Business*, September 25, 2018. https://www. crainsdetroit.com.

OpenCorporates. "Cousins Supermarket, Inc." https://opencorporates. com.

Page, Reverend Shelley. "History Happened Here." Unitarian Universalist Church of Flint. June 5, 2011. https://www.meadville.edu.

PBS NewsHour. "How and Why We Need to Get the Lead out of Our Lives." September 28, 2016. https://www.pbs.org.

Raymer, Marjory. "The Failed American Dream: Lessons from Flint's Civic Park Neighborhood." FlintSide, November 14, 2019. https://www. flintside.com.

Riddle, Tree. "Demolition Underway at Former Delphi Flint East Facility on Center Road." Banana 101.5. https://banana1015.com.

Smith, Ernie. "Lint, Filtered." Tedium. https://tedium.co.

Turner, Mike. "An Iconic, Historic Building Set to Begin Life Anew as Downtown Flint's Hilton Garden Inn." *AND Magazine*. September 16, 2020. https://and.flintandgenesee.org.

United States Census Bureau. *"Profile of General Demographic Characteristics: 2000. Geographic Area: Flint City, Michigan."* https://www.gc4me.com.

INDEX

A

AC Flint East 65, 66
AC Spark Plug 59, 60, 65, 103, 107
American Spiral Weld 131
Atwood Stadium 79, 80, 117, 118, 119
AutoWorld 52, 54, 72, 107, 133

B

Ballenger Manor 113, 114
Bijou Theatre 17
Brass Rail 51
Brooks and Penfield apartment buildings 42, 44
Bryant House 48
Buckler Beverage Company 72
Buick City 35, 61, 62, 63, 65, 70, 131, 132
Burning of the Greens 80, 81

C

Capitol Theatre 10, 18, 134, 135
Carriage Town 91, 117, 118, 125, 147
Chevy 44, 63, 66
Civic Park 83, 119, 120, 121, 122
Clark Commons 148
Clio Road 99, 102, 119
Coca-Cola 73
Community Service Center 25
Congregation Beth Israel 96, 97, 98

D

Dort Highway 60, 65, 67, 73, 75, 103, 104, 106, 107, 115
Doubie's 51
Dryden Building 51, 135, 136, 137
DuPont 69, 71

F

Fenton Building 17, 50
Fenton Hall 17
First Church of the Nazarene 92
First Congregational Church 88
Fisher Coldwater Road 61
Fisher One 60, 61
Flint City Hall 23
Flint Cultural Center 20, 21, 119
Flint General Hospital 84, 85
Flint Osteopathic Hospital 84, 113
Flint Park 31, 32, 87
Flint Public Library 10, 20, 21, 25,
    44, 111
Flint Sausage Works 70
Flint Water Crisis 10, 128
Floral Park 22, 33, 35, 39, 81

G

Garden Theatre 18
General Motors 16, 35, 42, 54, 59,
    60, 62, 63, 69, 94, 118, 119,
    127, 131
Genesee Bank 57, 109, 112, 120,
    139, 141
Genesee Memorial Hospital 84
Genesee Towers 18, 56, 58, 139
GM Powertrain Flint North 63, 65
GM Powertrain V8 Engine Plant
    65
Grand Trunk 41, 44, 119, 149

H

Halo Burger 43
Hat's Pub 51
Helmac 70
Hilton Garden Inn 141
Home Dairy Building 51
Hotel Dresden 26
Hubbard Hardware Complex 48
Hyatt Regency Hotel 46, 47, 142

I

IMA Auditorium 52, 53, 54

J

J.C. Penney 47, 48, 51, 136
J. Dallas Dort 16, 29, 69

K

Kearsley Park 80
Kewpee 43
Kresge Building 17, 50

L

Lakeside Park 30, 31
Lear Corporation 131

M

MacArthur Building 46
Majestic Theatre 17
Marketplace 59
McDonald Dairy 52, 71, 72
Milner Arcade 50
Milner Hotel 28
Mott Community College 20, 84,
    90, 138
Music Hall 17

N

North Flint Plaza 109, 111

O

Oak Grove Hospital 18, 20
Old East Side 86, 87, 115, 117

P

Paramount Potato Chips 67, 68, 69
Paterson Company 30, 54
Pengelly Building 30
Pepsi 72, 73
Perry Printing Company 52
post office 25, 136

Q

Quinn Chapel 21, 22

R

Rialto Theatre 26, 46
Royal Theatre 46

S

Savoy Theatre 26
Sherman Building 139, 141, 142
Sill Building 49
Smith-Bridgman Building 50
Smith Village 124, 125, 126, 148
South Flint Plaza 109, 111
St. Agnes 94, 95
St. John Street Neighborhood 35,
    39, 71, 82, 89, 94, 115
St. Joseph Hospital 84, 85
Stone's Opera House 17

T

Taystee Bread 41, 42
Temple Beth El 96, 97, 98
Thompson's Flowers 41
Thompson's Shopping Center 111,
    112

U

University of Michigan 21, 24, 25,
    26, 41, 47, 52, 56, 77, 107,
    119, 133, 142
University Park 122, 123, 124, 126

V

Voyager Inn 44, 55, 56

W

Walsh Building 45
Walter Winchester Hospital 32
Water Street Pavilion 48, 51, 107,
    133
WFBE 20, 75
WFDF 73, 74
WFUM 77
Windmill Place 38, 107, 108
Woodside Church 89, 90, 91
WTAC 74
WWCK 74, 76

Y

YMCA 24, 58, 144
YWCA 41, 43, 58, 137

ABOUT THE AUTHOR

Photo by Ivonne Raniszewski

G ary Flinn is a product of the Flint Community Schools and a graduate of Mott Community College and Michigan State University and has lived in the Flint area for most of his life. His earliest writings were for Flint Central High School publications the *Tribal Times* and the *Arrow Head.* He also contributed articles for the *Uncommon Sense, Broadside, Your Magazine, Flint Journal* and *Downtown Flint Revival* magazine. He presently lives on Flint's west side.

Also by Gary Flinn from The History Press:
Remembering Flint, Michigan: Stories from the Vehicle City
Hidden History of Flint